A SHERLOCK CAROL

BY MARK SHANAHAN

A DPS ACTING EDITION PUBLISHED BY

BROADWAY
LICENSING GROUP

A SHERLOCK CAROL
Copyright © 2023, Mark Shanahan

All Rights Reserved

A SHERLOCK CAROL is fully protected under the copyright laws of the United States of America, and of all countries covered by the International Copyright Union (including the Dominion of Canada and the rest of the British Commonwealth), and of all countries covered by the Pan-American Copyright Convention, the Universal Copyright Convention, the Berne Convention, and of all countries with which the United States has reciprocal copyright relations. No part of this publication may be reproduced in any form by any means (electronic, mechanical, photocopying, recording, or otherwise), or stored in any retrieval system in any way (electronic or mechanical) without written permission of the publisher.

The English language stock and amateur stage performance rights in the United States, its territories, possessions and Canada for A SHERLOCK CAROL are controlled exclusively by Broadway Licensing, 440 Park Avenue South, New York, NY 10016. **No professional or nonprofessional performance of the Play may be given without obtaining in advance the written permission of Broadway Licensing and paying the requisite fee.**

All other rights, including without limitation motion picture, recitation, lecturing, public reading, radio broadcasting, television, video or sound recording, and the rights of translation into foreign languages are strictly reserved.

Inquiries concerning all other rights should be addressed to Creative Artists Agency, 405 Lexington Avenue, 19th Floor, New York, NY 10174. Attn: Steve David.

NOTE ON BILLING
Anyone receiving permission to produce A SHERLOCK CAROL is required to give credit to the Author as sole and exclusive Author of the Play on the title page of all programs distributed in connection with performances of the Play and in all instances in which the title of the Play appears, including printed or digital materials for advertising, publicizing or otherwise exploiting the Play and/or a production thereof. Please see your production license for font size and typeface requirements.

Be advised that there may be additional credits required in all programs and promotional material. Such language will be listed under the "Additional Billing" section of production licenses. It is the licensee's responsibility to ensure any and all required billing is included in the requisite places, per the terms of the license.

SPECIAL NOTE ON SONGS/RECORDINGS
Broadway Licensing neither holds the rights to nor grants permission to use any songs or recordings mentioned in the Play. Permission for performances of copyrighted songs, arrangements or recordings mentioned in this Play is not included in our license agreement. The permission of the copyright owner(s) must be obtained for any such use. For any songs and/or recordings mentioned in the Play, other songs, arrangements, or recordings may be substituted provided permission from the copyright owner(s) of such songs, arrangements or recordings is obtained; or songs, arrangements or recordings in the public domain may be substituted.

for Cate

A SHERLOCK CAROL was originally produced off-Broadway at New World Stages in New York City, opening on November 21, 2021. It was produced by Raymond Bokhour, Drew McVety, and Fred Lassen for Fat Goose Productions, Laura Z. Barket for Theatre Nerd Productions, and executive produced by Nathan Gehan and Jamison Scott for ShowTown Productions. ShowTown Theatricals was the general manager. It was directed by Mark Shanahan, the set design was by Anna Louizos, the lighting design was by Rui Rita, the original music and sound design was by John Gromada, the costume design was by Linda Cho, the hair and wig design was by Charles G. LaPointe, the fight choreography was by Seth Andrew Bridges, the assistant director was Camden Gonzales, and the stage manager was Jill Cordle Mont. The cast was as follows:

SHERLOCK HOLMES .... Drew McVety
EBENEZER SCROOGE .... Thom Sesma
DR. TIMOTHY CRATCHIT and others .... Dan Domingues
EMMA WIGGINS and others .... Anissa Felix
DR. WATSON and others .... Mark Price
THE COUNTESS and others .... Isabel Keating
Understudies .... Joe Delafield, Alexandra Kopko, Byron St. Cyr

A SHERLOCK CAROL was given a virtual presentation as part of Florida Rep's New Plays Festival (Greg Longenhagen, Artistic Director; Jason Parrish, Festival Curator) in November 2020.

A further virtual presentation was delivered as part of the Script-In-Hand Series of the Westport Country Playhouse (Mark Lamos, Artistic Director; Anne Keefe and Mark Shanahan, Series Curators) in January 2021.

A SHERLOCK CAROL is based upon characters created by Sir Arthur Conan Doyle and Charles Dickens.

DRAMATIS PERSONAE

SHERLOCK HOLMES. The World's Foremost Consulting Detective, in decline.

EBENEZER SCROOGE. Formerly a miser. One Christmas, Scrooge transformed into as good a man as the good old city ever knew. (Also is noted as A GHOSTLY VOICE.)

The Company

Actor One

DR. TIMOTHY CRATCHIT. Tiny Tim, all grown up. Now, a doctor at St. Bernard's Hospital for Children. He speaks with a more refined accent than his sister.

MR. TOPPER. The manager of the Cosmopolitan Hotel. A bit older, a bit pompous. Easily irritated. Supposedly a friend of Fred, Scrooge's nephew.

RALPH FEZZIWIG. A nervous, wiry young man. The misfit member of a proud family. Engaged to Fannie.

CONSTABLE BRADSTREET. A seemingly upstanding member of Scotland Yard.

Actor Two

EMMA WIGGINS. A good-spirited and brave 13-year-old, she is a former Baker Street Irregular.

FAN "FANNIE" GARDNER. Scrooge's grandniece. A refined young woman, she works backstage at the theatre in the Cosmopolitan Hotel. Engaged to Ralph Fezziwig.

INSPECTOR LESTRADE. Blustery, easily confounded member of Scotland Yard. He has grudging respect for Holmes.

MRS. WINDIGATE. A Scottish tavern-keeper and member of the Goose Club. Giggly, a whirlwind.

Actor Three

DR. WATSON. Sherlock Holmes' best and most loyal friend. The Boswell to Holmes' Johnson.

MRS. DILBER. Mr. Scrooge's housekeeper of over 30 years. An emotional creature with a connection to the spiritual realm.

HENRY BURKE. An Irish candlemaker, an old friend of Mr. Scrooge.

OLD JOE BRACKENRIDGE. The owner of Old Joe's in Covent Garden. Gruff, a born salesman.

Actor Four

CAROLER. A cheerful person in the street.

ELDERLY WOMAN. A London lady.

THE COUNTESS OF MORCAR. American. An old love of Holmes' who also goes by another name, Irene Adler.

MARTHA CRATCHIT. Tough and a bit lower-class than her brother. She is as smart and observant as any detective she might happen to meet.

MARY MORSTAN. Watson's elegant and brave wife.

ABIGAIL "ABBY" FEZZIWIG. Runs a business fattening geese for market. She is no-nonsense and direct—a proud member of the hardworking Fezziwig family.

NOTES

The script is written for six actors, though it can be performed by a larger cast if the director so chooses. Recorded music can be used for transitions and underscoring, or a live piano player might be useful depending on the production.

Regarding casting—this is a loose and playful mash-up, an adaptation of the works of two very traditional authors. The actors are inhabiting the "idea" of the iconic characters, and can be cast in any number of ways. The actors are, after all, only spirits—which, as the play states, are around us all the time, guiding our way. Age, ethnicity and gender are all up for grabs in the casting, as is the suggestion of the breakdown of roles.

Regarding scenery—it is best to use a minimum of sets and props and employ suggestive costumes pieces to tell the story. The script aims to celebrate not only the magic of Christmas, but the magic of theatre and the playmakers' imagination, above all!

A SHERLOCK CAROL

ACT ONE

A mostly bare stage. This is London, 1894.

An old-fashioned lamppost sits center, adorned with a Christmas wreath. It might almost seem to be...a Ghost Light. Snow falls lightly. Music plays from offstage as the actors enter, singing.

THE COMPANY.
*Ding dong merrily on high
In heaven bells are ringing*

> *The carolers move about, joyfully. From the flock, one man emerges. He is unkempt, poorly dressed for the weather, attired in shirt with rolled sleeves and a waistcoat. He is disgruntled. He is Sherlock Holmes.*

*Ding dong verily the sky
Is riv'n with angel singing
Gloria, hosanna in excelsis!
Ding dong verily on high
In heaven bells are ringing*

> *A crash of thunder.*

A GHOSTLY VOICE. *(Ominously.)* SHERLOCK HOLMES!

> *The actors freeze. Holmes staggers backwards, terrified.*

HOLMES. Moriarty is dead to begin with. Moriarty is dead. I say it again, emphatically so—

> *The other actors turn and address the audience.*

THE COMPANY. Moriarty was dead, to begin with.

ACTOR ONE. It's true.

ACTOR TWO. Without question.

ACTOR THREE. Dead as a doornail.

ACTOR ONE. Three years ago.

ACTOR FOUR. Professor Moriarty had plunged to his death over the Reichenbach Falls.

ACTOR ONE. Locked in battle with his mortal enemy—

ACTOR THREE. One Mr. Sherlock Holmes.

HOLMES. "The World's Foremost Consulting Detective."

ACTOR TWO. That's who he is, you know.

ACTOR THREE. Or at least, who he was.

ACTOR ONE. Holmes had survived the fall at Reichenbach.

ACTOR FOUR. And now he was back. Back in London. Back at Baker Street. Back at home.

HOLMES. Which is no home at all, if you want to know.

ACTOR TWO. Everything had changed. For one thing—

HOLMES. Moriarty was dead, to begin with. How could it be otherwise?

ACTOR TWO. To Holmes, Professor James Moriarty had been—

HOLMES. The greatest schemer of all time, the organizer of every devilry, the controlling brain of the underworld, the Napoleon of Crime. I should have died at Reichenbach, too. That would have been fitting…

ACTOR TWO. For without his nemesis—

HOLMES. There is nothing new under the sun.

ACTOR ONE. Now, usually a Sherlock Holmes story is recounted from the journals of Dr. John H. Watson, M.D.

ACTOR THREE. *(As Watson.)* I had called upon my friend Sherlock Holmes at our old lodgings in Baker Street on the morning of Christmas Eve. He had been in a fog since his return to London—

ACTOR ONE. But this is not to be that kind of story.

> *Holmes and Watson are at 221B Baker Street. Holmes sits in his chair, gloomily. The other actors watch the proceedings.*

HOLMES. Out upon a Merry Christmas!

WATSON. But Holmes, I regard Christmas as a sacred occasion.

HOLMES. There is no greater fool than one who shouts "Happy Christmas!" in a city throughout which the foulest of mankind lurks round every corner. I'd do anything—anything to avoid this merriment.

WATSON. Well, then come to my house for a party.

HOLMES. Anything but that. I'll thank you to leave me alone, Watson.

WATSON. Mrs. Watson is preparing a turkey. And, we shall toast the season with the finest bottle of Christmas spirits—

Holmes leaps up, agitated.

HOLMES. Spirits?

WATSON. Yes, a host of spirits!

HOLMES. I have no use for spirits. Of any kind, Christmas or otherwise. Watson, I understand you wish to return to gallivanting about London solving meaningless crimes, however those days are in the past.

WATSON. But Inspector Lestrade has a pile of unsolved cases on his desk.

HOLMES. But Moriarty is dead!

WATSON. To begin with, yes. But, there are other criminals. Perhaps a good old-fashioned murderer might do the trick! Eh? Or a blackmailer. Yes! Oh, a blackmailer would do wonders!

HOLMES. Don't be a fool. Without a worthy adversary, I am nothing. The Professor may as well have dragged me down with him. I am not the Sherlock Holmes you wish me to be.

WATSON. *(Softly.)* I am sorry to find you so resolute. And I admit I am gravely disappointed. I believed in our partnership… I believed in Holmes and Watson.

ACTOR TWO. For what is Watson without Holmes?

ACTOR FOUR. And what is Holmes without Watson?

HOLMES. I said good afternoon!

Holmes gestures for his old partner to leave. Watson wears a heartbroken smile.

WATSON. Merry Christmas, Holmes.

HOLMES. Bah.

Watson exits.

ACTOR FOUR. Now, the end of "Holmes and Watson" is as good a place as any to begin our tale. So, let us repeat, emphatically, that—

ALL. Moriarty was—

HOLMES. Dead to begin with! Yes! Yes, we know!

ACTOR THREE. This must be distinctly understood or nothing wonderful can come from the tale we shall relate for you tonight.

The company sets the scene of a restaurant.

ACTOR ONE. Once upon a time, of all the good days of the years, the very day of Christmas Eve—

ACTOR TWO. A cold, bleak, and biting day in which fog poured in at every keyhole and the city clocks chattered as they struck one o'clock—

ACTOR FOUR. A spirited wind swept down the Thames—

ACTOR THREE. Through the thoroughfares of Old London—

ACTOR FOUR. Past the halls of Scotland Yard and the Lord Mayor's house—

ACTOR TWO. Past Mrs. Hudson's lodgings at 221B Baker Street—

Holmes sits at a table. Alone.

ACTOR ONE. Following Sherlock Holmes to the doorstep of his usual melancholy tavern, where he sat, taking his usual melancholy meal, alone—

ACTOR THREE. Quite alone—

ACTOR FOUR. Alone for all the world to see—

ACTOR ONE. Hard and sharp as flint, was Holmes—

ACTOR TWO. Self-contained and solitary as an oyster. For, you see, the Great Detective…was haunted.

A GHOSTLY VOICE. *SHERLOCK HOLMES…*

Holmes stands.

HOLMES. I do not believe in ghosts.

ACTOR FOUR. And so begins our tale.

ACTOR ONE. A tale of Sherlock Holmes.

ACTOR TWO. A tale of Christmas.

ACTOR THREE. A tale which happened once upon a time—

ACTOR FOUR. Once upon a time—

ALL. *(Softly.)* Once upon a time, on Christmas Eve…

> *A Caroler (Actor Four) sings "Good King Wenceslas" outside the restaurant. Holmes exits into the street.*

HOLMES. Off with you! You sound like a bag of drowning rats.

CAROLER. Penny a song, sir! Everyone loves a Christmas Carol.

HOLMES. I. Do. Not. Off with you!

> *The caroler flees. A young woman in a bonnet, Emma Wiggins (Actor Two), tentatively approaches Holmes.*

EMMA WIGGINS. Mr. Holmes? Mr. Holmes! It is you! I thought it was! You're back!

HOLMES. What?

EMMA WIGGINS. Don't you recognize me? Emma Wiggins! From your Baker Street Irregulars!

HOLMES. Wiggins?

EMMA WIGGINS. Oh, I need your help, sir. My father's been arrested. Police say he's a thief! You've got to help him, sir!

HOLMES. If your father committed an offense then he must answer for his crime and pay the penalty in full.

EMMA WIGGINS. But he didn't do it! Won't you help? After all, you're Sherlock—

A GHOSTLY VOICE. *HOOOLMESSSSSS…*

> *Holmes braces himself.*

HOLMES. Who's there?

> *The voice fades.*

EMMA WIGGINS. Mr. Holmes?

HOLMES. Did you not hear that?

EMMA WIGGINS. You've got to help me, sir! Please!

HOLMES. Leave me be, Wiggins.

EMMA WIGGINS. But Mr. Holmes! My father!

HOLMES. I said leave me be!

EMMA WIGGINS. I thought we could always count on you, sir… I guess I was wrong.

She runs off.

HOLMES. Bah.

Holmes returns to the restaurant. A man (Actor One) is seated nearby.

THE MAN. If I'm not very much mistaken, you are Mr. Sherlock Holmes.

HOLMES. You are.

THE MAN. What?

HOLMES. Mistaken.

The man rises with some difficulty. He is supported by a cane. He approaches Holmes.

THE MAN. No, I'm quite sure you're him. Your landlady Mrs. Hudson said I might find you here.

HOLMES. I'll have a word with her.

THE MAN. Mr. Holmes, I know tonight is Christmas Eve and I wouldn't dream of disturbing you.

HOLMES. And yet you are.

THE MAN. Ha. Bit shorter than I imagined from Dr. Watson's stories in the *Strand Magazine*. Those accounts are what made me think you're the only person what can help me.

HOLMES. I deplore Watson's narratives. Testaments to inaccuracy. I bear no resemblance to the character in the *Strand Magazine*. Watson paints me as an eccentric and incurable addict in a deerstalker hat, with a fiddle, prancing about London with a comical pipe between my teeth. I wouldn't wear a deerstalker if my life depended upon it. Now, if you don't mind—

Holmes coughs violently. The man offers his scarf.

THE MAN. Here, now, take my scarf. You're hardly dressed for this weather, sir. You're shivering.

Holmes takes the scarf.

HOLMES. How much do you want for the scarf?

THE MAN. Consider it a gift. Merry Christmas.

HOLMES. ...Bah. What cause have I to be merry?

THE MAN. Well, what cause have you to be dismal? You've only just returned to London, as I understand it. I heard—

HOLMES. That I was dead?

THE MAN. Something to that effect. But now you're here.

HOLMES. So you believe in ghosts.

The man follows Holmes back to his table.

THE MAN. Perhaps I have reason to. There has been a murder, you see—

Holmes sits.

HOLMES. I'm very sorry but I cannot help.

THE MAN. But if only you knew—

HOLMES. On the contrary, I do know. I know everything about you and have since the moment I saw you.

THE MAN. Ah, yes, your powers of observation. My favorite part of Dr. Watson's stories. Would you...?

HOLMES. ...Very well.

(Quickly, but not rushed, gathering momentum throughout, gradually getting more agitated at the obviousness of it all.) You grew up in Camden Town, as is obvious from the remains of those distinct vowels you have worked so hard to dispel. You do a fine job of concealing it, but the traces are still there. You were sponsored at a fine school though you started late in childhood, probably about the time your severe medical condition was treated. A kidney disease, I'd wager. Your limbs were malformed as a child, perhaps until the age of seven or eight from the looks of your recovery. You, or rather your family endured a reversal of fortune and received assistance to treat your illness before it could prove fatal, which it no doubt would have been within a year. It is not a leap to surmise a benefactor of some sort must have executed this miracle, given your family's humble circumstances and the late treatment of your condition, and it is this benefactor who sent you to the school where your

masters attempted to eradicate the elongated a's and e's in your speech. The school made a great impact on you, for you work with children even today, evidenced by the chalk on your sleeve and the little illustrated book folded neatly in your left pocket. It even has your name on it. May I call you Timothy? Your last name is folded on the other side, Doctor. Oh, yes, you're a doctor, as evidenced by the stethoscope concealed beneath your collar... And lastly, the murder of which you speak...it was your benefactor who died, was it not?

> *The man, Timothy Cratchit, plops down in a chair next to Holmes, flabbergasted.*

CRATCHIT. Astounding. Your talents are remarkable.

HOLMES. It's an affliction, not a talent.

CRATCHIT. And how did you know it was my benefactor who died?

HOLMES. You winced at the mention of the word. And now, I wish you a good day, Doctor...

CRATCHIT. Cratchit, sir. Dr. Timothy Cratchit. But the children down at the Hospital call me by my childhood nickname. Tiny Tim. You may too, if it pleases you.

HOLMES. It does not.

CRATCHIT. I daresay, you remind me a bit of my benefactor, as he was once upon a time.

HOLMES. Are we finished?

CRATCHIT. My benefactor was found dead at his home this morning, Mr. Holmes. Must've died sometime last night, locked in his room. It has been quite a blow. Hard to believe he and I shall never speak again.

HOLMES. How I envy him.

CRATCHIT. Perhaps you've heard of my benefactor. He was a great man. A man whose story is as heartening to me as Christmas itself. His name, Mr. Holmes, was—

> *Scrooge appears, elsewhere.*

SCROOGE. Ebenezer Scrooge!

CRATCHIT. At one time, he was a hard-hearted man. A squeezing, wrenching, grasping, scraping, clutching, covetous old sinner was Scrooge!

SCROOGE. Bah Humbug!

CRATCHIT. But then, one night, a Christmas night, many years ago, he was transformed. He woke upon a Christmas morning with the spirit of a new man!

Scrooge yells to an unseen boy.

SCROOGE. You there! Young boy! What day is this?

CRATCHIT. After that, he became like a second father to me, became as good a friend, as good a man, as this city ever knew.

SCROOGE. Merry Christmas!

Scrooge disappears.

CRATCHIT. It's quite a story, actually.

HOLMES. Fascinating. Are we done?

CRATCHIT. I called upon him three days ago on the occasion of his birthday. He has been confined to a wheelchair as of late and his sight has dimmed, but we had a happy visit. The old fellow told me that he was soon to receive a valuable gift. A rather famous diamond, he said, called the Blue Carbuncle.

HOLMES. I've heard of it.

CRATCHIT. A present from an old friend—though he would not say who—in gratitude for the many good deeds Scrooge had done. Of course, old Scrooge decided to give it away, and told me he planned to change his will. But as yet, no new will has turned up. And then, he showed me a letter he received…

Cratchit slides a piece of paper across the table. Sherlock can't help himself. He reads it.

HOLMES. "YoUr GhoSts HavE ReTurNed. THis *WILL* be your lAst ChrIstmaS"

These words were cut from the agony column in *The Times*. A left-handed person trying to appear right-handed, as you can tell from the angle of the blade.

CRATCHIT. And the word "WILL" is in larger letters than the others. Of course, Mr. Scrooge laughed it off.

HOLMES. *(Suspiciously.)* Tell me, Dr. Cratchit. Did you suspect he had chosen you as the beneficiary of his new will?

CRATCHIT. Over the years Mr. Scrooge has been quite generous to the children of St. Bernard's hospital, and made sure no boy or girl would suffer as I once did.

HOLMES. Regarding his death. Were there any signs of foul play?

CRATCHIT. No. But... The note. The missing will. If he met his end unfavourably, I must know.

HOLMES. Yes. Mind you, old age can be the most cunning of murderers. Ask Scotland Yard for assistance. Lestrade is the best of a bad lot. If something has happened—

CRATCHIT. I've spoken to the police. They wouldn't entertain my suspicions after I discovered the body. The police said only that they would send someone round to fetch the remains.

HOLMES. And so you came to me. I'm sorry, Dr. Cratchit. But, at this time I am not able...

> *Holmes spies a cloaked figure seated at another table, back to him.*

I am not able to... I am...not...

CRATCHIT. Mr. Holmes?

> *Holmes, agitated, springs toward the figure.*

HOLMES. What do you want with me? Fiend!

> *It is an elderly woman (Actor Four). She screams.*

Forgive me, madame...

ELDERLY WOMAN. AH! And a merry Christmas to you! Heathen!

> *She hits him with her bag and storms out of the restaurant.*

CRATCHIT. Mr. Holmes? Mr. Holmes, are you all right?

HOLMES. I'm sorry, Dr. Cratchit. Very sorry, indeed.

> *He exits the restaurant into the street. Cratchit follows.*

CRATCHIT. Mr. Holmes! Mr. Holmes, sir! Please. Mr. Holmes, sometimes a man can tell a doctor things he wouldn't tell another soul.

> *Holmes stops in his tracks.*

HOLMES. Moriarty died at Reichenbach. I know without doubt that he is dead. And yet, I see him everywhere.

CRATCHIT. See him?

As Holmes explains, a series of Moriarty-like silhouettes appears in the ether. With each description, they turn to reveal an innocent face.

HOLMES. On a street corner. When I least expect it, there he is. Tuesday last, walking along the Strand. There! A figure in black, the familiar gait...

I catch up to him, only to find a banker on his way to dinner.

I pass a shop on the Edgware Road, and there—his face in the window.

A closer look and—it is only a butcher at work in his shop, carving a Christmas roast.

But, Moriarty is there, constantly...hiding in the shadows. But, of course, it isn't him. It is my obsession. I know this. How can any spirit walk the earth? And how can I live with his cursed memory...?

Cratchit takes him in, recognizing that a melancholy deeper than he might have guessed stirs within the detective.

CRATCHIT. Mr. Holmes. You are a haunted man.

HOLMES. Perhaps Moriarty has beaten me after all.

CRATCHIT. You are more like Scrooge than you know. He, too, experienced a haunting. But he let it change him for the better. I won't rest until I know the truth about his death. Will you help me?

Holmes is silent. And perhaps a bit ashamed.

Well, then. A Merry Christmas, sir.

Cratchit begins to go.

HOLMES. Doctor... Do you believe? In ghosts?

CRATCHIT. As a man of science, I am bound by reason.

HOLMES. Exactly! A ghost may be a symptom of indigestion, an undigested bit of beef. Why, there's more of gravy than—

CRATCHIT. But, I believe we are far more than the fragile bodies we are given at birth. There are spirits all around us, Mr. Holmes, guiding our way.

A pause.

HOLMES. Then, tell me, as a medical man, what do *you* believe happened to your Scrooge? What could make a man transform so?

CRATCHIT. It's a mystery, Mr. Holmes.

HOLMES. ...Doctor, I will accept your case.

CRATCHIT. Do you mean—?

HOLMES. Yes, the game is afoot.

> *A haunting Christmas carol plays. The company transforms the scenery to the front door of Scrooge's home.*

ACTOR FOUR. Foggier now and colder still.

That spirited wind we mentioned earlier? It follows Holmes and Cratchit down the winding streets—All the way to Scrooge's home. Nipping at their heels. A piercing, searching, biting cold. A dismal, sickly London fog, so thick, Holmes can hardly make out the path.

> *Holmes and Cratchit arrive at the doorway...*

See it now, the home of Ebenezer Scrooge.

HOLMES. Quite a gloomy place.

CRATCHIT. I'll wait for you across the street, Mr. Holmes. I don't wish to go in there and see the old man lying in his state. You understand, I'm sure.

> *He limps away.*

ACTOR FOUR. Now it is a fact that there is nothing at all particular about the door knocker of Old Scrooge's place. Holmes had seen hundreds like it on the doors of London. But how then to explain...?

> *The sound of twisting metal. The door alters its shape. A face appears in the knocker. It says, "Sherlock...Holmes..."*

HOLMES. What in blazes...?

> *Thunder! The door opens and Mrs. Dilber (Actor Three) appears, startled. The door has returned to normal.*

MRS. DILBER. Ahhh! Mercy! You scared the tar outta me, you did! And just who are you, you sneaky ol' hedge creeper?

HOLMES. The name is Holmes. Sherlock Holmes.

MRS. DILBER. The detective? I thought you were dead.

HOLMES. Not quite. Dr. Cratchit sent me. You are the housekeeper?

MRS. DILBER. Mildred Dilber. Loyal to Mr. Scrooge for thirty-five years and more. And now... Didja hear? Oh, it's too 'orrible fer words. It's Mr. Scrooge, y'know. He's...he's...he's...

HOLMES. Dead, yes. I know.

> *She weeps with a frightening wail and blows her nose into a hankie.*

MRS. DILBER. Oooh! Yes. Just inside. Isn't it terrible? Oh, the poor old flapdoodler. Everyone loved him so. Almost as much as they used to hate him. We shall not see his like again!

HOLMES. May I come in?

MRS. DILBER. Right this way.

> *She ushers him through the doorway.*

You can join the other fellow.

HOLMES. The other fellow?

> *Lestrade (Actor Two) blusters in the hallway, eating a piece of cake.*

LESTRADE. Mrs. Dilber, this cake is quite delicious. Just one question—

HOLMES. Hello, Lestrade.

LESTRADE. Well, well, well. The rumors are true. Mr. Sherlock Holmes is back. And where's Dr. Watson, then? Off writing one of his stories, hoping to make the police look like buffoons?

HOLMES. I'm no longer working with Dr. Watson.

LESTRADE. Ha! You don't say? You know, I heard you were dead.

HOLMES. I've heard that, too.

MRS. DILBER. Not feelin' well? Would you like a piece of me cake, Mr. Holmes? I always bake when I'm upset.

HOLMES. If the taste resembles the pungent odor which permeates this hall, no thank you.

MRS. DILBER. But—it's m'famous choc'late amaretto!

HOLMES. Mrs. Dilber I didn't come here to partake of stale cake, I am here because a man may have been murdered.

MRS. DILBER. Murdered! Dash m'wig, is it true?

LESTRADE. Don't mind him, Mrs. Dilber. Thinks he's better'n everyone. Why're you really here?

HOLMES. A courtesy call.

LESTRADE. Scotland Yard has been doing quite well on my own—on *OUR* own!—without *you*, you know.

HOLMES. I've spoken to a Dr. Cratchit who believes the dead man may have met a premeditated end.

LESTRADE. Pish! He died of old age. He was ancient as a fossil.

HOLMES. And yet something bothers you.

LESTRADE. ...Cratchit said there was a note.

HOLMES. And a missing will, yes I know.

LESTRADE. Always one step ahead, aren't you?

HOLMES. Where is the body?

LESTRADE. In the study. But I've already seen everything in there.

HOLMES. You see, but you do not observe.

MRS. DILBER. Ahhh! Nonononono. Don't disturb the body! I tell you, I can feel him. He's not...crossed over yet. Mr. Scrooge's spirit lingers still. He's with us even now.

HOLMES. His spirit?

MRS. DILBER. Of course, Mr. Holmes. Don't you believe? There are spirits everywhere. Keepin' watch. You'd best be careful.

> *Holmes enters the study. He takes a magnifying glass from the mantle and surveys the room. A carol such as "God Rest Ye Merry Gentlemen" plays in a decidedly minor key. A Victorian, high-backed wheelchair faces away from us, an arm lying stiffly from its side, a newspaper clutched in hand. Actor Four narrates Holmes' investigation.*

ACTOR FOUR. Now, the rooms throughout Scrooge's house are spare and cheerless.

HOLMES. Ah.

ACTOR FOUR. With many items missing.

HOLMES. Hmmm.

ACTOR FOUR. For, even in the years after his transformation, Old Scrooge—

HOLMES. Never spent a penny on himself.

ACTOR FOUR. The hallways are long and dark.

But the study is different. It is cheerful, adorned with flourishes of Christmas decor. Were it not for the sadness of the occasion, the study would make the perfect setting for a yuletide party.

MRS. DILBER. This is where Old Scratch did most of his living.

LESTRADE. And most of his dying.

HOLMES. Sh!

ACTOR FOUR. And there, tucked comfortably into his wheelchair, sits the body of one—

HOLMES. Ebenezer Scrooge.

ACTOR FOUR. A thin smile traced upon his lips. Scrooge's face is angled to the wall, where hangs the gentle portrait of a young woman in a bonnet. On the frame is written a name—

HOLMES. Fan.

ACTOR FOUR. On the opposite wall, a bookcase, filled with adventure stories.

HOLMES. *Don Quixote, Robinson Crusoe, David Copperfield.*

ACTOR FOUR. And there, a day bed.

HOLMES. Undisturbed.

ACTOR FOUR. With a plump pillow bearing a monogram with a fancifully curled letter—

HOLMES. "S."

ACTOR FOUR. In the dead man's hand, a copy of the *London Times*—

Holmes pries it from the dead man's grip.

HOLMES. December 22nd edition.

ACTOR FOUR. Open to page three. On the writing table, several Christmas cards, neatly stacked.

LESTRADE. I've already looked through those.

ACTOR FOUR. And, an advert for a Christmas Eve performance

at the Concert Hall of the Cosmopolitan Hotel, a program of carols to be performed by—

HOLMES. The Countess of Morcar. Of course.

MRS. DILBER. Who's she?

HOLMES. Hold this.

> *He tosses Mrs. Dilber the magnifying glass. She catches it, startled. Holmes wipes a finger on the spot of the floor near the window.*

ACTOR FOUR. Though the room is cold and damp, the walls and tables of the study are lined with pewter candlesticks, all of them melted entirely to the base, reminding one that here, in this room, a great light once burned brightly, but now had been extinguished.

> *The music ends. Actor Four exits.*

LESTRADE. He's dead all right.

HOLMES. Rather sharp bit of detective work on your part, Inspector.

LESTRADE. What do *you* make of it all?

HOLMES. The floor is disturbed. Here.

MRS. DILBER. Beg y'pardon?

LESTRADE. I don't see it.

HOLMES. No, you don't.

MRS. DILBER. Wasn't my doing.

HOLMES. But you're the housekeeper.

MRS. DILBER. Retired last year. But I keep busy. Volunteer down at Dr. Cratchit's hospital Tuesdays, work the soup kitchen for the Temperance Society Wednesdays—

HOLMES. Yes—but what were you doing here this morning?

MRS. DILBER. I'm loyal to me old boss. Still come in now and again to help with the linens and cooking. And provide a bit of company. I don't like the thought of him being alone at his age. And this being Christmas Eve and all, I come by with to bake a cake.

LESTRADE. Delicious, too. Chocolate almond. My favorite is apple, of course, and—

HOLMES. Thank you, Lestrade. You came this morning, Mrs. Dilber?

MRS. DILBER. Nine o'clock, shortly before Dr. Cratchit. We figgered Old Scratch been sleeping late in his study. I found a spare key, we open the door, and there's the old flubber in his chair. Dead.

LESTRADE. As a doornail. No weapon or marks on the body.

HOLMES. The door was locked? There's no key on Scrooge.

LESTRADE. No sign of a struggle, either. Only thing that bothers me is that note and the missing will.

MRS. DILBER. Perhaps, we should hold a seance? Contact him on the other side? I'm well acquainted with summoning spirits. I'm a conduit!

LESTRADE. I think Scotland Yard can handle this without a seance thank you very much. We'll take the body to the morgue and let you know if anything turns up.

From out back, a scream! Somewhere, a window shatters.

HOLMES. Quick, Lestrade! Out back!

Holmes and Lestrade run from the house, through the open door and into the street.

LESTRADE. This fog! I can't see a thing!

HOLMES. This way, Lestrade!

LESTRADE. Holmes!

HOLMES. Follow me!

LESTRADE. Holmes, where are you?

HOLMES. Over here, in the alley!

Cratchit stumbles out of the fog.

CRATCHIT. Mr. Holmes?

He collapses to the ground. A hat and a large sack containing a goose lie beside him.

HOLMES. Dr. Cratchit!

LESTRADE. He's dead!

HOLMES. For goodness sake, Inspector. He's not dead.

LESTRADE. Oh, right.

Cratchit stirs.

CRATCHIT. Good job, I'm not, though.

HOLMES. Can you stand?

CRATCHIT. Yes, thank you.

HOLMES. What happened?

CRATCHIT. I was across the street, and I saw a tallish man wearing this hat, walking along, carrying a white goose slung over his shoulder. Then a smaller fellow come from the alley and a row broke out.

Holmes looks about.

HOLMES. The smaller one attacked the man in the hat and you rushed forward to help, correct?

CRATCHIT. Yes, I raised my cane and swung it over my head.

HOLMES. Smashing the window behind you in the process.

CRATCHIT. They must've thought I was brandishing a weapon of some sort.

HOLMES. And seeing Lestrade's wagon from Scotland Yard, they both took to their heels and vanished.

CRATCHIT. The small bloke got a swipe in first.

HOLMES. Leaving you with a battered hat, and a most unimpeachable Christmas goose.

CRATCHIT. Which surely must be restored to its rightful owner.

LESTRADE. We haven't a clue as to his identity.

HOLMES. We have his hat.

LESTRADE. Lots of men have hats like that.

HOLMES. But only a few bear the initials "H.B." Doctor, have you quite recovered?

CRATCHIT. Yes, thank you.

HOLMES. And, where will you take your Christmas Eve supper?

CRATCHIT. At St. Bernard's hospital. My sister Martha always cooks a holiday meal for the children.

HOLMES. Can Miss Cratchit cook a goose?

CRATCHIT. She can.

HOLMES. Then take it to her.

CRATCHIT. But what of the fellow who lost it?

HOLMES. Unless we find "H.B." in a matter of hours, which is highly doubtful, the bird will go to waste.

CRATCHIT. This attack happened outside Mr. Scrooge's house. Do you think the event is connected to his death?

HOLMES. Go to your hospital, Doctor. I shall handle this affair on my own. Do you understand?

CRATCHIT. I do, sir.

Holmes puts the hat on his own head.

LESTRADE. Be honest, Holmes. Is there a murderer on the loose?

HOLMES. Inspector. There's always a murderer on the loose.

LESTRADE. And where're you off to, now?

HOLMES. Me? I'm going to investigate—a Christmas carol.

The scene changes to a theatre. A curtain rises and a woman (Actor Four) appears in a spotlight. She is the Countess of Morcar, wonderfully elegant and grand with a hint of a mischievous, wild spirit lurking below the surface. She is dressed in an exquisite gown, with accents appropriate for the season. A small orchestra is in the midst of playing a jaunty selection. She is enjoying her audience. They are in the palm of her hand.

THE COUNTESS. Is everyone having fun tonight?

The audience cheers!

Oh! You're a lovely audience!

She picks up the music and sings!

Here we come a-caroling
Among the leaves so green,
Here we come a-wand'ring
So fair to be seen.
Love and joy come to you,
And to you your wassail, too,
And God bless you, and send you
A Happy New Year,
And God send you a Happy New Year.

On the twelfth day of Christmas

My true love gave to me,
Twelve drummers drumming,
Eleven pipers piping,
Ten Lords a-leaping,
Nine ladies dancing,
Eight maids a-milking,
Seven swans a-swimming,
Six geese a-laying,
Five golden rings!

…One moment. One moment, please.

> *She falters, looking out into the crowd. The musicians hold for her, momentarily confused. She spots someone in the back of the auditorium.*

Well, well, well.

> *The Countess cues the little orchestra to start again.*

Four calling birds
Three French hens
Two turtle doves, and
A partridge in a pear tree!

> *She finishes with some fanfare. Applause!*

Thank you. That will be all! And a very Merry Christmas to you!

> *She goes to her dressing room, backstage. Fannie (Actor Two), her young dresser, helps her. The Countess sits at a vanity and wipes her makeup. She has an American accent.*

FANNIE. Quite a show tonight, Countess.

THE COUNTESS. Thank you, Fannie. I thought to finish a bit early.

FANNIE. Are you all right, ma'am? There were two songs left, I believe.

THE COUNTESS. Yes, yes, I'm fine. I was just… I thought I saw an old friend in the audience, and it rattled me just a bit.

> *Holmes barges in, followed by Mr. Topper (Actor One), a whiskered man who is the manager of the theatre. The Countess stands.*

MR. TOPPER. Excuse me! You can't come back here! This is a private dressing room!

THE COUNTESS. It's all right, Mr. Topper. Let him in. This is Mr. Sherlock Holmes.

FANNIE. The famous detective?

MR. TOPPER. I heard he was dead.

THE COUNTESS. ...So did I.

MR. TOPPER. Excuse me, Countess. I didn't realize he was your guest.

THE COUNTESS. It's all right, Mr. Topper. Civilians aren't normally allowed backstage. But Mr. Holmes is a special case. Might we have a moment alone?

FANNIE. As you wish, ma'am.

MR. TOPPER. I'll be right outside if you need me. Right outside.

Fannie and Topper exit. Sherlock and Countess stare at each other for a moment before breaking into furtive grins. The Countess laughs with giddy joy. There is a history here that is undeniable, deep and palpable.

THE COUNTESS. Ha! So, you're alive! I didn't believe the rumors, of course. Though, I'm sure it's quite a story. I take it Moriarty is dead?

HOLMES. To begin with.

THE COUNTESS. You look like a ghost yourself. Are you ill?

HOLMES. I'm… I've been better.

THE COUNTESS. Ah. I see.

He changes the subject. She lets him.

HOLMES. And what of you?

THE COUNTESS. Oh, Sherlock… You know me. I always manage to land on my feet.

HOLMES. You've married again?

THE COUNTESS. You can't expect me to wait around for my true love to come to his senses and propose.

HOLMES. A Count this time? Rather a step down from the King of Bohemia.

She picks up a small framed photograph propped on her vanity and smiles at it with true fondness.

29

THE COUNTESS. The late Count of Morcar was a very sweet and generous man. And I truly adored him. I did.

He gave me my title, bless him. And a lot of money. Lends my act a little respectability, you know.

HOLMES. The title suits you. Otherwise you'd still be known simply as Irene Adler, of Trenton, New Jersey.

THE COUNTESS. *(Grandly.)* Yes, well. Irene Adler doesn't have as polished a reputation as—the Countess of Morcar!

HOLMES. But I'm told she can hit some remarkably high notes.

THE COUNTESS. *(Coy.)* You ought to know.

> *She lets out an infectious laugh and Holmes momentarily melts just a bit.*

OH! It's good to see you again, my sweet. In fact, I could use your help.

HOLMES. The Blue Carbuncle?

THE COUNTESS. How did you know?

HOLMES. That it's missing? I saw a picture of you on stage in Vienna last year. It was in the setting of that very necklace. The jewel you wear now is quite lovely, of course—

THE COUNTESS. And real.

HOLMES. But it isn't the Blue Carbuncle. You intended the Carbuncle as a gift for Ebenezer Scrooge, but it has since been stolen.

THE COUNTESS. Scrooge will be terribly upset when he finds out.

HOLMES. No, he won't. My condolences.

> *The gravity of his words hits her.*

THE COUNTESS. Oh. Oh, no. Dear Ebenezer…

> *She turns away, visibly moved. Holmes is caught off guard by the depth of her reaction.*

HOLMES. Were you close to Mr. Scrooge?

THE COUNTESS. I was.

HOLMES. Part of your checkered past?

THE COUNTESS. I was young. Fell in with the wrong crowd, you might say. I owed a substantial sum and my life was threatened. I was introduced to Ebenezer. One night, he caught me in the act of stealing some money. His money.

Scrooge appears, elsewhere. He is kindly and concerned.

SCROOGE. My dear Miss Adler.

THE COUNTESS. I was ashamed.

SCROOGE. You should have told me.

THE COUNTESS. I had nowhere else to turn. I had no choice.

SCROOGE. We always have a choice.

THE COUNTESS. He didn't call the police. Instead, he gave me the money. As a gift.

SCROOGE. A small matter, to make you so full of gratitude.

THE COUNTESS. I had never known such kindness.

SCROOGE. There is nothing in the world so hard as poverty, dear girl. I wish for you a changed nature, an altered spirit, and a sense of Hope.

THE COUNTESS. I promised to pay it back, of course!

SCROOGE. And I release you from that contract. Remember this kindness and offer to help someone else one day. It is never too late to change. May you be happy in the life you choose!

Scrooge disappears, though the warmth of his presence lingers.

THE COUNTESS. He saved my life, without question. I owe him everything.

HOLMES. And that's why you intended to gift him the Blue Carbuncle? To repay him?

THE COUNTESS. Ebenezer believed people could change. I wanted him to see that he was right.

The Countess opens the door.

Fannie? Mr. Topper? Will you come in?

She leans in to Holmes.

Say nothing of Ebenezer's death. No offense, Sherlock, but your bedside manner's a bit lacking.

Fannie and Mr. Topper enter.

Mr. Holmes, this is my dresser, Francine Gardner. Fannie is the daughter of Mr. Scrooge's nephew, Fred.

HOLMES. I've seen a portrait of your grandmother, Fan, in Mr. Scrooge's study. You look remarkably like her.

FANNIE. I'm told Uncle loved her more than anything in the world.

THE COUNTESS. And this is Mr. Topper, the manager of the Cosmopolitan Hotel.

MR. TOPPER. And an old friend of Fan's father, Freddie, my former business partner, who lives in America, now.

HOLMES. Are you in Mr. Scrooge's debt, too?

MR. TOPPER. Excuse me, sir?

THE COUNTESS. We all owe a great deal to Ebenezer. Although Fannie isn't on speaking terms with her uncle at the moment. Fannie, will you tell him? It's important.

FANNIE. My Uncle Ebenezer recently told me of a change to his will. I wanted him to know I'd never ask for a penny of his money, but I was desperate for his support. You see, my father doesn't approve of my engagement to Ralph.

HOLMES. Ralph?

FANNIE. Ralph Fezziwig, a young man I've known since childhood. Uncle likes Ralph, of course. He's known the Fezziwigs for years. But Uncle insisted he wouldn't interfere and speak to Father on my behalf. He says it was not his place.

MR. TOPPER. That is because Ralph Fezziwig is a musician, Fan. *(With horror.)* A…myoo…sician! No father wishes his daughter to such a creature!

She ignores Topper.

FANNIE. Ralph plays violin in our orchestra. You'd like him.

MR. TOPPER. Your father merely wishes you to marry someone more stable, perhaps a bit older. Someone with a sure hand in business.

Fannie charges Topper.

FANNIE. Mr. Topper, I've told you before, I am not flattered.

MR. TOPPER. Well, I hope you won't regret your decision!

She turns quickly back to Holmes.

FANNIE. If only Uncle would intervene! I went to see him late last night to make amends, but when I saw him through the window of his study, I didn't have the courage to knock.

HOLMES. Countess, what does this domestic drama have to do with the Blue Carbuncle?

THE COUNTESS. Yesterday, I was to personally deliver the Carbuncle to Mr. Scrooge. As a present. The jewel was here in my dressing room under lock and key. In the morning, Mr. Topper asked a hotel employee named Bill Wiggins to come in to repair a window.

HOLMES. Wiggins?

MR. TOPPER. I came back later. Wiggins was gone.

THE COUNTESS. And so was the diamond.

The drawer had been forced open.

MR. TOPPER. Wiggins was arrested several hours later.

THE COUNTESS. But the stone couldn't be found.

FANNIE. I know Mr. Wiggins well and I cannot believe he's a thief.

MR. TOPPER. The man fainted when they arrested him, protesting his innocence.

HOLMES. But you're satisfied of his guilt, Mr. Topper?

MR. TOPPER. Wiggins had a previous conviction, you see. And if he has stolen from my hotel—

THE COUNTESS. The Cosmopolitan's reputation is intact, Mr. Topper. That will be all, for now.

MR. TOPPER. Yes. For now!

He exits, muttering to himself.

FANNIE. Mr. Holmes. You're a man of renown. I hope you can recover the diamond and clear Mr. Wiggins. Perhaps, too, you could speak to Uncle on my behalf. Ralph is, after all, my true love.

She leaves.

THE COUNTESS. She's young. She doesn't know yet. With true love comes—

HOLMES. A partridge in a pear tree.

THE COUNTESS. That was Ebenezer's favorite Christmas carol. No, I was going to say with true love comes a certain amount of heartache. Perhaps you can help them, in some way? You are, after all, the Great Sherlock Holmes.

HOLMES. Am I?

THE COUNTESS. Oh, you really are lost this time, aren't you, my love? I'm leaving London by steamer tomorrow morning. A Christmas voyage. My next engagement is in Australia. If you do manage to find the Blue Carbuncle, I trust you to know what to do with it. That diamond has a history. Just like us.

She kisses him, tenderly.

HOLMES. Do you think Scrooge was right? Can people really change?

THE COUNTESS. Perhaps one day, we'll put his theory to the test. In the meantime, I'd better tell Fan the news of her uncle.

HOLMES. Then this is goodbye.

She takes his hand, gently.

THE COUNTESS. For now. Merry Christmas, Mr. Holmes. I hope you catch the spirit.

She leaves. Holmes is alone. He picks up a small, handheld mirror on the vanity and looks at himself. A darkness descends. He shuts his eyes.

A GHOSTLY VOICE. *Holmes...*

HOLMES. No... I do not believe...in ghosts.

The voice turns to a cackle. Holmes rushes from the dressing room.

ACTOR ONE. Back to the streets.

ACTOR THREE. Back to the fog.

ACTOR ONE. Back to the cold. Down this lane and that.

ACTOR THREE. Following the tracks of wheels and wagons, the furrows that cross and recross each other hundreds of times—

ACTOR ONE. Intricate channels, hard to trace in the thick yellow mud of the pavement...

Holmes stops.

HOLMES. There is someone following me.

He continues though a maze of crooked lanes.

ACTOR ONE. Now, a different street. An empty street. The house fronts here look black enough, the windows blacker still.

ACTOR THREE. The sky is dark. There is no Christmas here. There is nothing here. Not a soul. Or is there?

> *Holmes hides in a doorway. A hooded figure scurries forward. Holmes leaps out and confronts his mysterious pursuer.*

HOLMES. Show yourself!

> *The figure's hood drops. It is Emma Wiggins.*

EMMA WIGGINS. Mr. Holmes! It's only me!

HOLMES. Emma? Emma Wiggins. You were following me?

EMMA WIGGINS. Yes, sir. Sorry, sir. I went to the Cosmopolitan Hotel to investigate on my own, to clear my father's name—but then I saw you! You're on the case, aren't you?

HOLMES. No, no, now Emma—

EMMA WIGGINS. Oh, Mr. Holmes, thank you! I knew you wouldn't let me down.

> *The wind picks up. Holmes begins to cough.*

HOLMES. Go home, Emma.

EMMA WIGGINS. But, I have nowhere to go. My father was all I had in the world. Without him I'm lost. And quite hungry, sir. What am I to do?

HOLMES. Follow me.

> *A carol plays as the company sets up a little Christmas party at St. Bernard's Hospital. A small, feebly decorated Christmas tree. A table and chairs. A locked medical cabinet.*

> *Holmes and Emma speak privately to Dr. Cratchit in his office.*

CRATCHIT. Of course you can stay tonight at St. Bernard's, Emma. You'll have a proper Christmas dinner, too. My sister's preparing a goose!

EMMA WIGGINS. Will there be potatoes, Dr, Cratchit?

CRATCHIT. There will be, Emma! And a bit of puddin' too, I shouldn't wonder. Now go join the others.

EMMA WIGGINS. Thank you, sir.

> *She scurries off.*

CRATCHIT. She'll be cared for here, Mr. Holmes. Though I'm not sure how much longer our doors will remain open. We're in dire straits, I'm afraid.

HOLMES. A sizable inheritance from Mr. Scrooge would help matters, no doubt.

CRATCHIT. ...Mr. Scrooge was always more than generous to this hospital.

HOLMES. I see.

Holmes coughs violently. Cratchit turns to the medicine cabinet.

CRATCHIT. That's a rather nasty cough, Mr. Holmes. Let me fetch you something.

HOLMES. Quite an apothecary you have, there.

CRATCHIT. I keep my cabinet locked tight. Too many robberies, I'm afraid. One just last week. There's all sorts of dangerous mixtures in here. Laudanum, morphine, cocaine...

HOLMES. I'll forego my usual seven-percent solution and take the other half of that bottle of cyanide on the top shelf.

CRATCHIT. Never joke like that to a doctor, sir. Every life is precious. Have a knock of this.

He gives Holmes a glass.

HOLMES. But this is merely—

CRATCHIT. Brandy yes. From my own personal supply. Cheers.

Holmes downs it. Cratchit joins him in a drink.

HOLMES. Now, to business.

He tosses his hat to Cratchit.

CRATCHIT. What?

HOLMES. The hat of Mr. H.B. You know my methods, apply them.

CRATCHIT. Very well. Now, then. Errr. To begin with. It's obviously. An old...hat?

HOLMES. Brilliant.

CRATCHIT. I give up.

HOLMES. Try again.

CRATCHIT. Red silk lining. Discolored. No maker's name. Initials scrawled inside. The elastic is missing!

HOLMES. Better.

CRATCHIT. Dusty, spotted in places, some attempt to hide the worn patches with ink. Other than that, I see nothing.

HOLMES. Disappointing.

CRATCHIT. What am I missing?

Holmes snatches the hat and places it on a table.

HOLMES. The owner was highly intellectual, and fairly well-to-do within the last three years, although he has fallen upon hard times. He drinks too much which may account for the fact that his wife no longer loves him.

CRATCHIT. Come now. I only have one good leg to pull, Mr. Holmes.

HOLMES. He has retained some degree of self-respect, leads a sedentary life, is middle-aged, has grizzled hair recently cut, and uses lime-cream.

CRATCHIT. Oh, now surely—

HOLMES. Also, it is extremely unlikely that there is gas laid on in his house.

CRATCHIT. All right, then. One by one. What makes you think the man was intellectual?

Holmes holds up the hat for inspection.

HOLMES. It is a question of cubic capacity. A man with so large a brain must have something in it.

CRATCHIT. Oh, please. And his fortunes?

HOLMES. The hat is three years old. If he could afford to buy such an expensive hat three years ago, and has had no hat since, then he has assuredly gone down in the world.

CRATCHIT. And his drinking?

HOLMES. He has enough self-respect to cover the whiskey stains on the felt with ink. That he is middle-aged is clear by the large number of gray scissor-cut hair ends, and there is a faint odor of lime-cream along the lining.

CRATCHIT. And his wife?

HOLMES. This hat has not been brushed for weeks. He's exhausted his wife's affections.

CRATCHIT. Perhaps he's a bachelor?

HOLMES. His ring finger has cut into the felt on this side.

CRATCHIT. And the gas?

HOLMES. One tallow stain, even two, might come by chance—I see five. He's brought into frequent contact with burning wax—he walks upstairs at night with his hat in one hand and a candle in the other.
Are you satisfied, Watson?

CRATCHIT. Cratchit, sir.

HOLMES. I beg your pardon?

CRATCHIT. You called me Watson.

HOLMES. I did not.

CRATCHIT. Mr. Holmes. Perhaps you'd like a second opinion from a more familiar doctor?

> *Martha Cratchit (Actor Four) enters. She is a bundle of energy and in high dudgeon! She carries a goose on a platter. There is great warmth between the brother and sister.*

MARTHA. Timmy! Oh, Timmy! It's the goose! The goose! You've got to see it!

CRATCHIT. Mr. Holmes, allow me to introduce my dear sister, Martha.

HOLMES. Miss Cratchit.

MARTHA. Hallo, hallo, hallo. Timmy! Who's your handsome friend, then?

CRATCHIT. Martha, this is Sherlock Holmes!

MARTHA. Sherlock Holmes, eh?

CRATCHIT. Yes. The famous detective.

MARTHA. Never 'eard of him.

CRATCHIT. Martha!

MARTHA. And is there a *Mrs.* Sherlock Holmes?

CRATCHIT. You'll have to forgive my sister, Mr. Holmes!

MARTHA. Why for? He's obviously not married, he's got no ring on his finger! And I'll wager he hasn't got a lady in his life, as evidenced by his lack of concern for his general appearance. Though he's a man of some means as he likes to travel—his shirt is an Italian make, and those kind of shoes are only sold in Switzerland, if I'm not mistaken.

CRATCHIT. I say, maybe you two should get to know each other, after all.

HOLMES. Thank you just the same.

MARTHA. All right, all right! Don't have to be such a Scrooge about it.

HOLMES. Excuse me?

CRATCHIT. Martha has never quite taken to Mr. Scrooge. She remembers him from a time before his change.

HOLMES. You don't believe in Mr. Scrooge's redemption?

MARTHA. If a man can turn over a new leaf that quickly, he can always turn back. Some people don't change.

HOLMES. I wonder.

MARTHA. Oh… I see. You've already found true love, but your heart's been broken. Just my luck. The interesting ones are always unavailable!

CRATCHIT. Martha—

MARTHA. If she is "The Woman," go after her! True love is hard to come by. Believe me.

CRATCHIT. Martha, please! Apologies, Mr. Holmes. Now, what of the goose?

MARTHA. Oh, yes. The goose! I nearly forgot. See here! Lookit what I found in its crop while I was preparing the bird! Is this a thing?

She holds out her palm, revealing a brilliant blue stone.

HOLMES. By Jove, Miss Cratchit! This is "a thing," indeed.

CRATCHIT. Mr. Holmes, is that…?

HOLMES. It most certainly is. The Blue Carbuncle.

MARTHA. Lord have mercy! Wait… What's a Blue Car-frumple?

HOLMES. Carbuncle, Miss Cratchit. A rare stone, found in the banks of the Amoy River in southern China. It has a sinister history. There have been two murders, a suicide, and several robberies for the sake of this forty-grain weight of crystallized charcoal. This pretty toy recently found its way into the hands of an old friend. It was she who planned to make a gift of it to Ebenezer Scrooge.

CRATCHIT. Will you return it to her?

HOLMES. She has asked me to take care of the matter myself. Emma Wiggins' father was arrested yesterday for stealing the bauble.

MARTHA. Is Wiggins guilty?

HOLMES. I highly doubt it.

CRATCHIT. And what of "H.B."?

HOLMES. Probably an innocent man, with no idea the value of the bird he carried.

CRATCHIT. If only we knew the identity of the hat's owner!

MARTHA. This hat here?

CRATCHIT. Martha, please—

HOLMES. Yes, Miss Cratchit, if you could just—

MARTHA. Oh! Pipe down, the both of you! I've seen this hat before.

HOLMES. Have you?

MARTHA. I'm sure of it. The funny little stains and everythin'? You can tell a lot about a man from his hat.

HOLMES. Indeed, Miss Cratchit!

MARTHA. You're looking for a middle-aged man with a sullen wife—

HOLMES. Yes! A man who is taken to drink—

MARTHA. And is highly intelligent—

HOLMES. A man who has fallen on hard times—

MARTHA. And uses a candle—

CRATCHIT. A man who has the initials—

HOLMES, MARTHA, and CRATCHIT. H.B.!

MARTHA. Oh, yes! That's right. That'd be Mr. Burke's hat, it would! Fits the description perfectly.

CRATCHIT. Henry Burke?

HOLMES. Who, pray tell, is Mr. Henry Burke?

MARTHA. A friend of Mr. Scrooge. Owns the little candle shop by Arthur Court. Comes to read to the children on Tuesdays.

HOLMES. Are you sure of this, Miss Cratchit?

MARTHA. As sure as I'm Tiny Tim's sister!

CRATCHIT. Mr. Holmes, Martha is never wrong!

MARTHA. And what ya gonna do with that shiny little diamond?

HOLMES. Until the missing will turns up, I shall hold on to it. For now, I must pay a visit to Henry Burke.

He puts on the hat.

MARTHA. Ya can't go out like that in this weather! Here, take a spare coat.

She gets him a black coat.

HOLMES. Thank you, Miss Cratchit, you've been most helpful.

The Cratchits gasp and freeze at the sight of Holmes, now clad in a flowing coat, a hat, and a scarf.

(Taken aback.) What is it?

CRATCHIT. That coat belonged to Mr. Scrooge, at one time.

MARTHA. You look quite like him, you know.

HOLMES. Do I?

MARTHA. It's like looking at a ghost.

HOLMES. Bah.

Holmes turns and leaves. The company dismantles St. Bernard's.

ACTOR TWO. Christmas Eve fast approaches, though it has been quite dark all day. The many passers-by hustle to and fro as Holmes edges along the crowded paths of life, making a brief stop for a crucial purchase—

HOLMES. The goose in the window. Be quick about it.

Actor Two hands Holmes a large burlap bag.

ACTOR TWO. Though the cold is intense, holly sprigs and berries crackle in the heat of the shop windows, making Holmes' pale face ruddy as he passes by, until at last he reaches—

A small shop. A frail-looking and woozy man, Henry Burke

(Actor Three), an Irishman, is lighting a candle. He turns, startled by the sight of Holmes in the doorway.

HOLMES. The Olde Chandlery, Henry Burke Proprietor.

BURKE. What?! Is it you? I thought you were dead.

HOLMES. I beg your pardon, my name is—

BURKE. Scrooge! Sure, and I knew you'd be coming back. Why, it just wouldn't be Christmas without you, now.

HOLMES. What? No, sir. My name is Sherlock Holmes.

BURKE. Sherlock Holmes?

HOLMES. Mr. Burke, steady yourself.

Holmes takes the man by the arm. Burke squints.

BURKE. You're not Scrooge after all, are you? Oh, no.

He holds back a tear. His knees buckle.

HOLMES. Come by the fire, sir. It is a cold night.

BURKE. Forgive me. I mistook ya for someone else, I did. A friend o' mine. Ebenezer Scrooge. They say he died this morning.

HOLMES. I'm afraid it's true.

BURKE. Fair dues like, I was jus' dozing in the back room—dreaming about him. And then I come out and see your man in the door dressed like that…

HOLMES. A slight trick of the mind.

BURKE. I been taking a little swig, too. A bit o' jolification. But don't tell the wife.

HOLMES. Mr. Burke, is this your hat?

BURKE. It is! But I thought sure I'd lost it when—

HOLMES. When you paid a visit to Mr. Scrooge, carrying a large goose as a present.

BURKE. That's right. Was Mr. Scrooge helped me open this candle shop when I came from Dublin without hardly a penny. Every year I bring him a fine goose for Christmas as a thank-you. But today—

HOLMES. You were attacked by some ruffians and lost both your bird and your hat.

BURKE. An expensive goose, too. But I was happy to spend a portion o' what savings I have lately on Mr. Scrooge.

HOLMES. The hat, I return to you. As for the goose, I was compelled to eat it.

BURKE. To eat it? D'you mean…it's gone?

HOLMES. Yes. However, I do hope a replacement goose might satisfy you? Will the one in this pouch do?

BURKE. Oh, it will, sir. It will.

HOLMES. Of course, I still have the feathers, legs, and crop of your original bird, if you wish to have them.

BURKE. I can hardly see what use the disjecta membra of my old goose might be to me. No, sir, with your permission, I will bring home that fine bird you have there.

HOLMES. Excellent answer. Here you are. Your wife will be quite pleased, no doubt.

BURKE. My wife has been never quite pleased with anything, sir. Believe me.

HOLMES. And might I ask where the other bird came from? I am somewhat of a fowl fancier myself.

BURKE. There are a few of us who frequent the Alpha Inn, near the museum. This year our hostess, Mrs. Windigate by name, instituted a wee goose club.

HOLMES. A…goose club?

BURKE. For a few pence every week, we each receive a bird at Christmas. My pence were duly paid, and the rest is familiar to you.

HOLMES. I see. Good afternoon.

BURKE. I have nothing to give you in return for your kindness.

HOLMES. Oh, I—

BURKE. Would you like a candle? Made to order—whatever scent you wish! This one's from Scrooge's last batch, in fact! And there you are.

> *He opens a box and offers Holmes a white candle with red stripes. Holmes holds it awkwardly.*

HOLMES. No gifts, please. I must be—

BURKE. Then keep the hat. It's all I can offer. But, Scrooge always considered even the smallest gift to be important. "It all adds up," he would always say. The ghosts taught him that. But of course, you would know all about Ghosts.

HOLMES. Would I?

BURKE. He'd talk about it to anyone who would listen, now, wouldn't he? How the Ghosts of Christmas had taught him his lessons. Were you a close, personal-like friend of his?

Holmes falters. The wind picks up.

HOLMES. No. But I wish that I could talk to the man just now. I have questions.

BURKE. Well, then, talk to him. Some spirits answer, don't you know? No one's ever really gone. Certain folk, if they have a hold on us, they stay with us forever, even after they've passed.

Holmes fumes.

HOLMES. What do you mean by that? What ineffable twaddle!

BURKE. Oh no, sir. Ghosts are real! It's quite certain.

The wind picks up. A wheezing, rattling sound echoes.

HOLMES. *(Angrily.)* The only thing certain is that you are a fool who knows nothing of the matter. I should never have taken this case. Ghosts and missing diamonds. My business here is done!

BURKE. I'm sorry, Mr. Holmes. I only meant—

HOLMES. To what?

BURKE. …to wish you a Merry Christmas.

HOLMES. Bah!

Holmes, in full Scrooge regalia, exits into the street. Thunder rumbles. "God Rest Ye Merry Gentlemen" plays.

ACTOR ONE. A bitter night!

ACTOR TWO. A bit of snow!

ACTOR FOUR. No Christmas for this tortured soul.

ACTOR TWO. His footfalls ring down Wimpole Street—

ACTOR ONE. Down through Wigmore, into Oxford, and on and on—

ACTOR FOUR. Lost in a maze of empty passageways.
HOLMES. Baker Street! I must return to Baker Street.
ACTOR FOUR. His breath blows like so many pistol shots—
HOLMES. Is someone there? Who is following me? Is it you?
The wind howls.
ACTOR ONE. The sky is darker now.
ACTOR FOUR. And the wind grows stronger.
ACTOR TWO. His mind's been torn, he knows not how—
HOLMES. I can go no longer.
ACTOR TWO. His thoughts are a tempest. Confusion sets in.
A rumble of thunder. A large shadow appears in the snowy street—a silhouette of a man wearing a cloak, hat, and walking stick.
HOLMES. Who is there! Show yourself!
A crack of thunder and lightning. The shadow approaches. Holmes falls to his knees.
Is it you? Moriarty, is it you? I do not believe in ghosts!
Another crack of thunder! The figure steps forward. It is—
Scrooge?
SCROOGE. Bah, Humbug! HA HA HA!
Blackout!

End of Act One

ACT TWO

The same as before. A crack of lightning.

SCROOGE. Boo.

HOLMES. But—I saw you. Dead.

SCROOGE. As a doornail, yes.

HOLMES. Who are you?

SCROOGE. Ask me who I was.

HOLMES. No. My… My mind is torn to pieces.

SCROOGE. Come here, and know me better, man.

HOLMES. I will not! You are a figment of my imagination.

SCROOGE. Why do you doubt your senses?

HOLMES. Because…your very existence is impossible.

SCROOGE. When you have eliminated the impossible, whatever remains, however improbable…

HOLMES. Must be…the truth. So, am I to believe that you are the Ghost of Ebenezer Scrooge?

SCROOGE. I prefer the term "spirit." And I daresay you are in dire need of some spirit, Mr. Holmes.

HOLMES. Bah. What business do you have with me?

SCROOGE. My business is your welfare! And your reclamation.

HOLMES. I shall take care of that myself. No Ghosts need apply.

SCROOGE. I am very much afraid for you, my boy. You are now as I once was. Oh, how I used to wag my finger and curse the heavens, and say—

> *In a flash, the world becomes dark and foreboding as Scrooge slips into his old persona.*

If I could work my will, every idiot who goes about with "Merry Christmas" on his lips, should be boiled with his own pudding and buried with a stake of holly through his heart!

> *The foreboding air passes.*

That was the old me. Sound familiar? But it doesn't have to be you.

You can change, you know. You must turn back from your present course before it is too late. Take heed!

HOLMES. I will not! I do not believe in you. For if you exist, then so must—

SCROOGE. Professor Moriarty?

> *In the distance, there is a faint death rattle—the whisper of a final breath.*

HOLMES. Indeed. He was the greatest schemer of all time, the organizer of every devilry, the Napoleon of—

SCROOGE. Oh, you do go on about him.

HOLMES. You don't understand. There is no use for a Sherlock Holmes…if Moriarty is dead.

SCROOGE. Which he most certainly is. Moriarty is condemned to wear the chains he forged in life, link by link. His spirit is doomed.

HOLMES. He deserved his fate. Perhaps I shall share it.

SCROOGE. Oh, I see, now… You're not afraid of death. You're afraid of life.

HOLMES. Why shouldn't I be? I know the horrors of this world. I have looked directly upon the horrors others choose to look away from.

SCROOGE. You fear the world too much and credit it too little.

HOLMES. I have seen Murderers. Thieves. Criminal masterminds. Prisons and workhouses overflowing with those I helped jail! And yet I live in a world of fools, eyes closed as the world spins into madness. They waste their hours on pointless holidays, singing wretched songs and exchanging gifts and—

SCROOGE. You're wrong. Christmas is a kind and charitable time. A season of forgiveness. As for gifts, you have been given gifts in abundance, m'boy.

HOLMES. And if I choose not to use them that is my business!

SCROOGE. Mankind is your business! The common welfare is your business! You are Sherlock Holmes. It is your business to know what other people don't.

HOLMES. You're an idealist, Scrooge. Just like Watson.

SCROOGE. Well, I admit, I've read all of his stories. Bit of a fan, you might say. Starting with that very first one published in *Beeton's Christmas Annual*. "A Study in Scarlet"!

HOLMES. Watson's stories belong to a different time of life. That's all in the past.

SCROOGE. Yes. Your past. Don't you remember?

> *Watson appears, elsewhere. He does not look at Holmes. A wistful carol plays.*

WATSON. "How are you?" he said cordially, gripping my hand with a strength for which I should hardly have given him credit. "You have been..."

> *Holmes is drawn to the memory.*

HOLMES. "...to Afghanistan, I perceive."

WATSON. "How on earth did you know that?" I asked in astonishment.

> *Holmes takes in Watson, as if for the first time. A memory.*

HOLMES. And I said... Here you see a gentleman with the air of a military man. An army doctor. He has come from the tropics, for his face is not his natural tint. He has undergone...hardship and sickness. His left arm has been injured. He holds it in a stiff and unnatural manner. He had seen so much...hardship.

WATSON. Afghanistan, yes! I wondered at first if he was as friendless a man as I was myself. We were both looking for—

HOLMES. Lodgings.

WATSON. Comfortable rooms—

HOLMES. At a reasonable price.

WATSON. 221B Baker Street! He warned me of his shortcomings, stating—

HOLMES. *(As if confessing to something forgotten.)* I get in the dumps at times, Watson. I don't open my mouth for days on end. You must not think I am sulky when I do that. Just let me alone, and I'll soon be all right. We might as well know the worst of each other if we are to become—

> *Watson turns to Holmes. They make eye contact.*

WATSON. Friends.

HOLMES. Friends. Yes. I never had a friend before.

Watson opens a small writing book.

WATSON. From the journals of Dr. John H. Watson, M.D. *The Adventures of Sherlock Holmes*!

Actors One, Two, and Four enter, playing many distinctly different characters from the Sherlock Holmes stories. Perhaps they do not even change costumes as they embody the parade of names.

ACTOR TWO. Mr. Holmes, my name is Helen Stoner—

ACTOR ONE. Dr. Grimesby Roylott.

ACTOR FOUR. Lord Backwater.

ACTOR ONE. Jabez Wilson—

ACTOR FOUR. Mary Morstan…

ACTOR TWO. Mycroft Holmes.

ACTOR ONE. Wilhelm von Ormstein!

ACTOR FOUR. Mrs. Hudson.

ACTOR TWO. Sir Henry Baskerville!

ACTOR ONE. Cecile Stapleton.

ACTOR FOUR. Irene Adler.

ACTORS ONE, TWO, THREE, and FOUR. Please, Mr. Holmes—I need your help!

HOLMES. I know them, Spirit! I know them all!

They vanish. Watson is left behind.

WATSON. Sherlock Holmes. My friend. The best and wisest man I have ever known.

Watson vanishes.

SCROOGE. What troubles you?

HOLMES. I should like to say a word or two to my old assistant just now.

SCROOGE. Didn't you call him a fool?

HOLMES. He may not himself have been luminous, but he was always a conductor of light. But, he is better off without me. He has Mrs. Watson, Mary, now, in any case.

SCROOGE. Indeed he has.

> *Mary Morstan (Actor Four) enters. It is Christmas Eve. The Present.*

MARY. John? Is that you?

SCROOGE. In fact he is with her at present.

WATSON. Yes, Mary.

MARY. Did you see him?

WATSON. I did.

MARY. And will he come?

WATSON. He won't. I fear we have lost him, Mary. For good, this time. He no longer resembles the man I knew. He wishes to have nothing to do with me.

MARY. More shame for him, John.

WATSON. His offenses carry their own punishment, and I have nothing to say against him.

MARY. Well, I do! I have no patience with him. You two were friends!

WATSON. I suppose that is the way in life. People go their separate paths. How fortunate I am to have you.

MARY. I'll always be with you, my love. Still, I know how he bothers you and so it bothers me.

WATSON. Who does he hurt, really? Only himself.

> *Mary coughs.*

My word. Still coughing, Mary?

MARY. I'm fine, love. Fine.

HOLMES. She's unwell. Oh, Mary. Mary, I didn't know. Spirit, if something were to happen to her, Watson would be…

SCROOGE. Alone, yes.

MARY. You are a dear man, John Watson. Put Sherlock Holmes out of your mind. Come, it's Christmas Eve!

> *They exit.*
>
> *Tim Cratchit appears, elsewhere. He sees Emma at a window.*

SCROOGE. Christmas Eve. Everywhere. Tonight.

CRATCHIT. Can't you sleep, Emma?

EMMA. No, Dr. Cratchit.

CRATCHIT. I can't either.

EMMA. I heard you tell Mr. Holmes the hospital is in danger of closing. Is that why you're awake?

CRATCHIT. ...It is. And I'm sure you must be thinking about your poor father.

EMMA. Yes, sir. But Mr. Holmes is on the case, isn't he? He's sure to solve the mystery. He always does.

CRATCHIT. I'm sure Mr. Holmes will do all he can. That is to say, all that he is able to.

EMMA. Do you think Mr. Holmes is unwell, sir?

CRATCHIT. I believe he is troubled.

EMMA. I believe so, too. I'll pray for him. God bless him, sir.

Cratchit is moved by the young girl's compassion.

CRATCHIT. Indeed, Emma. God Bless us, everyone.

They vanish.

A church bell chimes. Scrooge is silent. He suddenly looks withered, solemn. His face disappears beneath his hat.

HOLMES. You have shown me the past and the present, Scrooge. I fear to ask. What will you show me next? Say something, man!

Scrooge points a bony finger towards a vision of an elderly Watson, holding flowers. He is bundled against a howling wind and stands before a grave. Emma, approaches. She is older, too.

EMMA. Dr. Watson? Is that you?

HOLMES. This is the future, is it not?

WATSON. Who's there?

EMMA. Emma Wiggins, sir. From long ago. Don't you remember me?

WATSON. Oh, yes. Wiggins. That's right. Of course. Wiggins.

EMMA. Merry Christmas, sir. Who are you here to visit, Doctor?

WATSON. ...My dear wife is laid to rest here. Lost her many Christmases ago, now.

EMMA. I was paying my respects to Dr. Cratchit, he's beneath that tree. Do you remember him?

WATSON. Cratchit, yes. Used to run a hospital for children. Closed up, didn't it?

EMMA. It did. Dr. Cratchit cared for me after my father died in prison. Poor Father never had his name cleared.

WATSON. Bah. Scotland Yard. I hear it's worse than ever since they promoted Lestrade to Chief Inspector.

HOLMES. Oh, dear Lord.

WATSON. We always knew he had no talent.

EMMA. Doctor. What ever happened to…to Sherlock Holmes?

WATSON. Oh, he's among these stones somewhere, I think. He was…a disappointment. Haven't heard his name in years. I never understood how he could have fallen so far. But then, perhaps some mysteries have no solutions.

EMMA. I sometimes wonder, what if—

WATSON. No. Don't. Banish those words from your mind. "What if?" We will never know "what if." Forget about Sherlock Holmes, Miss Wiggins. I have.

They part. Watson walks by Holmes and for a moment it seems he looks right at him, though not on an earthly plane…

HOLMES. Watson?

WATSON. …He wasn't the man I thought he was.

Watson exits. Holmes turns to Scrooge.

HOLMES. Scrooge, tell me! Are these the shadows of things that will be? Or are they the shadows of things that may be only? What would you have me do, Spirit?

SCROOGE. It is not for me to say, Sherlock Holmes. Men's courses will foreshadow certain ends, to which, if persevered in, they must lead.

HOLMES. But if the courses are departed from—

SCROOGE. Then the ends may change.

HOLMES. I fear I am past all hope.

SCROOGE. Waste your gifts at your own peril. And risk the welfare of all those who would care for and rely upon you in years to come. No, sir, it is not too late! You may change these shadows with an altered life and a thankful heart.

HOLMES. But without Moriarty—

SCROOGE. You do not need Moriarty to be Sherlock Holmes. Your greatest adversary is yourself, man!

HOLMES. Then what must I do? To be well and truly changed? To rid myself of despair?

SCROOGE. You must care for your brothers and sisters! You must use your gifts as they were intended! You must do what you were always meant to do. You must be Sherlock Holmes and—

HOLMES. Solve a mystery.

SCROOGE. Exactly, man! Now do it! Solve the mystery surrounding my death. Find out—

HOLMES. Who stole the Blue Carbuncle. And why...

SCROOGE. You know the suspects. You've heard their stories. You've seen the clues. It all adds up. In fact, I believe deep down you already know the solution, don't you?

HOLMES. Of course I do.

SCROOGE. And how is that possible?

HOLMES. Because, I am Sherlock Holmes!

SCROOGE. Then prove it, you ol' Humbug! Remember all that has passed between us! The game is afoot! Ha ha!

With a crack of lightning and the deafening ring of a bell, Scrooge vanishes. Holmes is alone on the street. Light snow.

ACTOR ONE. The fog is lifted, now. The cold night air snaps Holmes back to his senses.

ACTOR FOUR. He must have been dreaming. He is a man of rational thought.

ACTOR ONE. He cannot, he will not, he does not—

HOLMES. Believe in ghosts.

ACTOR FOUR. ...Or does he?

ACTOR ONE. Still, if he has been sleepwalking, he now finds himself exactly where he needs to be.

He looks up. A sign for the Alpha Inn.

HOLMES. The Alpha Inn.

ACTOR FOUR. A small public house on Holborn Street.

Carols play on an accordion. A wonderful, boisterous Christmas party is underway. A Scottish landlady (Actor Two) appears. She is having the time of her life.

MRS. WINDIGATE. Mrs. Windigate, at yer service, dearie. How kin I help you? …Halloo??

HOLMES. Ah, yes. Yes. Of course.

MRS. WINDIGATE. A wee drinkie, for a Merry Christmas, now!

HOLMES. Thank you. Is your beer as good as your goose?

She turns and pours a beer, talking over her shoulder.

MRS. WINDIGATE. My goose?

HOLMES. Yes, I was speaking only half an hour ago to a member of your goose club.

MRS. WINDIGATE. Ach, yes! But you see, sir, those aren't my geese.

HOLMES. Whose then?

MRS. WINDIGATE. I got the two dozen from a salesman in Covent Garden.

HOLMES. Indeed? Which one?

MRS. WINDIGATE. Brackinridge is the name. Old Joe Brackinridge. Ha! Here y' are—

HOLMES. Thank you, Mrs. Windigate.

MRS. WINDIGATE. Ach! Wait! Whattabout yer wee drinkie?

HOLMES. You've been most helpful, indeed!

He exits as Mrs. Windigate hoists the beer!

MRS. WINDIGATE. Ach! The more for me! Happy Christmas!

The company sets up Covent Garden.

HOLMES. Onwards.

ACTOR FOUR. To the south. With a quick march—

ACTOR ONE. Across Holborn—

ACTOR FOUR. Down Endell—

ACTOR ONE. Round the corner—

ACTOR FOUR. Through a zigzag of slums—

ACTOR TWO. Racing faster now. Until finally he reaches—

ALL. *Covent Garden!*

> *Covent Garden appears as the actors call out like vendors, talking over each other.*

ACTOR TWO. Pies! Pies of every variety! Get your Christmas pies here!

ACTOR ONE. GOOD KING WENCESLAS LOOKED OUT, ON THE FEAST OF STEPHEN—thank you, sir!

> *Holmes gives a shilling to the caroler. Blending in.*

ACTOR THREE. Bric-a-brac! Secondhand goods at cut-rate prices! Bric-a-brac! Bric-a-brac!

ACTOR FOUR. Calling birds! French hens! Turtle doves!

ACTOR TWO. Figgy Pudding! Bring home some figgy pudding!

> *Holmes arrives at a stall with a shingle—"Old Joe's, Whatever you want, Old Joe can get." A man in an apron and multiple scarves (Actor Three) is closing up shop. He's rough, a born salesman.*

HOLMES. A cold night.

OLD JOE. 'Tis.

HOLMES. Have you any geese?

OLD JOE. Sold out. Let you have a hundred geese tomorrow morning.

> *He opens his overcoat, the inside lined with spoons, baby shoes, and other trinkets.*

Just now, how's about some bed curtains or spoons or shoes. Anything you want, Old Joe's got.

HOLMES. What I want is a goose.

OLD JOE. Try the other stalls, then.

HOLMES. Ah, but I was recommended to you. By a woman at the Alpha Inn.

OLD JOE. Aye. I sent her a couple dozen.

HOLMES. Fine birds. Where did you get them?

OLD JOE. Here, now. What're driving at?

HOLMES. I'd like to know who sold you those geese.

OLD JOE. Oh, would ya now? Well I shalln't tell you! How d'ya like that for a Merry Christmas!

HOLMES. No need to get hot.

OLD JOE. You'd be hot too if you were pestered as I am today. It's "Where are the geese?" and "Who did you sell the geese to?" and "What do you want for the geese?" You'd think they were the only geese in the world, the fuss some people make.

HOLMES. But I bet my friend a fiver the bird I ate was country-bred.

OLD JOE. Then you lost your bet. That bird was town-bred.

HOLMES. I don't believe it.

OLD JOE. You think you know more about fowls than I, do you? I say, all those birds that went to the Alpha were town-bred. Bet another fiver on it?

HOLMES. I'd merely be taking your money. I know that I am right.

> *Old Joe opens a ledger. A rat-faced man (Actor One) appears in the shadows, pretending to be shopping at another stall.*

OLD JOE. Lookee here, then, Mr. Cocksure. You see this? That's the list of the folk from whom I buy. On this page, the country folk, and this page the town folk. Read that name, there.

HOLMES. Miss Abigail…Fezziwig. 117 Brixton Road. Twenty-four geese.

OLD JOE. And sold to Mrs. Windigate of the Alpha. Now pay up!

HOLMES. I'm chagrined. Another question. I see among your secondhand bric-a-brac those spoons.

> *He reaches inside Joe's overcoat and effortlessly snatches a spoon.*

Monogrammed with a fancifully curled letter "S." I know the man who once owned them. How did they come into your possession?

OLD JOE. Here now, what're accusing me of? I get bundles coming in all the time. And I don't ask the origins. I've had those spoons nearly a year with no questions.

HOLMES. I see. Lastly, do you know the man over my shoulder who has been so clumsily eavesdropping upon us?

OLD JOE. Oy! He's another one! Coming round about the geese!

Old Joe shouts to the man, who is startled.

I told you, I don't know where your goose went! Pester me again, either of you, and I'll set the dog on you! Merry Christmas. Bric-a-brac!

Old Joe exits. The rat-faced man darts past the stall and Holmes grabs him by the arm.

HOLMES. A word, my good man.

RAT-FACED MAN. What do you want?

HOLMES. I think we're here for the same reason.

RAT-FACED MAN. You can't know a thing about—

HOLMES. My name is Sherlock Holmes. It is my business to know what other people don't.

RAT-FACED MAN. Not about this.

HOLMES. You are endeavoring to trace some geese which were sold by a woman from Brixton Road, are you not?

RAT-FACED MAN. Oh, sir. My apologies. You are the very man I've longed to meet.

HOLMES. We need privacy. Come.

They step into a secluded alley beneath a lamppost. The man sits on a wooden crate.

Before we go any further. Give me your name.

RAT-FACED MAN. Robinson…Jack Robinson.

HOLMES. No, no. Your real name, please. It's so troubling to do business with an alias.

RAT-FACED MAN. …Fezziwig. Ralph Fezziwig.

HOLMES. Just so. Young Fezziwig. The violinist at the Cosmopolitan Hotel. Fiancé to Fan Gardner.

RALPH FEZZIWIG. How did you—

HOLMES. You wish to know what became of those geese?

RALPH FEZZIWIG. I do.

HOLMES. Or rather, of a particular goose. White, with a black stripe across the tail?

RALPH FEZZIWIG. Oh, sir! Can you tell me where it went?

HOLMES. It went with me. And a remarkable bird it was. It laid the brightest little blue egg that ever was seen. I have it here.

> *Holmes reveals the Blue Carbuncle in his hand. Ralph stands, transfixed. After a moment, he lunges at Holmes, violently. Holmes defends himself easily and makes quick work of Ralph, who lands in a heap on the ground.*

The game is up, Fezziwig.

RALPH FEZZIWIG. Oh Lord, Oh Lord, Oh Lord…

> *Holmes extends a hand and quickly helps Ralph off the ground. Fezziwig is awash in regret as he sits on a crate.*

HOLMES. How did you know of the Countess' blue stone?

RALPH FEZZIWIG. My fiancée. Fannie. She'd seen it. But she had nothing to do with my taking it, I swear.

HOLMES. I believe that. You knew suspicion would fall on the hotel worker Wiggins. You made a small job of the dressing room window and Mr. Topper sent for Wiggins. When Wiggins had left, you rifled the jewel case, raised the alarm, and Wiggins was arrested. You then—

> *Ralph throws himself to the floor.*

RALPH FEZZIWIG. For God's sake, have mercy! Think of my good family's name! Of my beloved grandfather, Dear Old Fezziwig who practically raised me! I don't want to shame his mem'ry! I never went wrong before! I never will again. I swear it. Oh, don't bring me into court!

HOLMES. It is well to cringe and crawl now.

RALPH FEZZIWIG. I will fly and leave the country, Mr. Holmes. The charges against Mr. Wiggins will collapse.

HOLMES. …Confess.

RALPH FEZZIWIG. Yessir. I wanted to get away from the hotel with the stone. I was afraid the police would search me as I'd been spotted near the dressing rooms. I made for my sister Abby's house. She lives in Brixton Road, where she fattened birds for market. I was in a panic.

Abigail Fezziwig (Actor Four) appears, elsewhere.

ABBY FEZZIWIG. What's wrong, then, Ralphie? You comin' down with something?

RALPH FEZZIWIG. Been a jewel robbery at the hotel, Abby. Upset me a bit.

ABBY FEZZIWIG. Ah. Go into the yard. Smoke yer pipe.

RALPH FEZZIWIG. I went out back among her geese to think. I had a friend, spent hard time in Pentonville. He said he could get rid of stolen goods. I decided to go to him and turn the stone into money.

HOLMES. But you feared you might be seized and searched. You saw the geese about your feet. And an idea came into your feeble head.

RALPH FEZZIWIG. I thrust the stone down the neck of one of the birds, one with a striped tail, as far as my finger could reach. The bird gave a gulp and flapped out of my hands.

Abigail Fezziwig appears again.

ABBY FEZZIWIG. Whatcha doing with that bird, Ralphie?

RALPH FEZZIWIG. You said I could have one for Christmas. I was just choosing the fattest.

ABBY FEZZIWIG. I set you one aside.

RALPH FEZZIWIG. Well, if's all the same. I'd rather have that white one there, with the funny tail.

ABBY FEZZIWIG. Suit y'self. Take it with you. We'll see you tomorrow night for the Fezziwig family Christmas party. And don't be late, this time.

RALPH FEZZIWIG. I did what she said, and carried the bird to my friend. He got a knife and opened the goose. My heart turned to water. There was no sign of the stone. I rushed back to my sister's but there was not a bird to be seen.

ABBY FEZZIWIG. They all gone to the dealer's Ralphie.

RALPH FEZZIWIG. Which dealer?

ABBY FEZZIWIG. Old Joe's in Covent Garden.

RALPH FEZZIWIG. Were there two with the same tail, Abby?

ABBY FEZZIWIG. Yes, Ralph. Two striped-tail ones. Never could tell them apart. What in heaven's name is wrong, Ralph?

She exits.

RALPH FEZZIWIG. And now, I am branded a thief. Without ever touching the wealth for which I sold my character and sacrificed my fiancée's love. I'm a disgrace to the good old name Fezziwig!

> *He falls to his knees sobbing and drops his pipe. There is a long pause.*

HOLMES. …Go.

RALPH FEZZIWIG. What, sir? Oh heaven bless you!

HOLMES. I said go!

> *Ralph flees, terrified and relieved. Holmes picks up the pipe and regards it, curiously. He is reminded that such a pipe feels a natural fit in his hand. He sits on the crate and listens to the sound of carolers singing "Hark the Herald Angels Sing" in Covent Garden.*

(*Quietly.*) Are you there, Scrooge? Can you hear me? "If a man has committed a crime, he must pay the price in full…" My very words, were they not?

But then, what is the price of saving a soul? I let Ralph Fezziwig go rather than make a jailbird of him for life. The fellow's too frightened to go wrong again.

And, you did say this was a season of forgiveness, did you not?

Ha. If Watson could see me now. Talking to ghosts.

And yet, there is still more to do this Christmas Eve.

Oh, yes.

There is still the matter of your peculiar death, Old Man.

I know the suspects. I've heard their stories. I've seen the clues.

"It all adds up."

> *The company sets up Scrooge's chambers as before, complete with empty wheelchair facing upstage. The actors chant, to a drum beat. Wind picks up.*

ACTORS ONE, TWO, and FOUR.
Twelve drummers drumming
Eleven pipers piping

Ten lords a-leaping
Nine ladies dancing
Eight maids a-milking
Seven swans a-swimming
Six geese a-laying
Five golden rings,
Four calling birds
Three French hens
Two turtle doves

HOLMES. And a partridge in a pear tree.

Holmes disappears into the darkness, unseen. Sleigh bells (Slay bells?) are heard in the distance.

The door to the chambers opens. A draped figure enters, leaving the door ajar. A shaft of light spills into the room. The figure creeps in and rummages through a drawer. It rips open a pillow and searches the stuffing.

The door slowly closes with a click. The figure turns around to see the shadow of a man in a black coat and top hat standing silently at the door. The figure reacts in shock and speaks, revealing herself to be Mrs. Dilber.

MRS. DILBER. Who's there? Speak!

Silence.

No, it can't be. You're dead. I saw you. It can't be you, Mr. Scrooge.

The shadow lights a match, revealing Holmes. He is oddly cheerful, slightly playful, even.

HOLMES. Why not, Mrs. Dilber? Don't you believe in ghosts?

MRS. DILBER. Mr. Holmes. What's the meaning of this? You scared me half to death!

Holmes lights a white candle with red stripes, but conceals its distinct look from Mrs. Dilber with his hand.

HOLMES. We'd best be careful with the other half, then. Because it is on account of the dead that I have come here tonight. I'm very glad to see you, Mrs. Dilber.

MRS. DILBER. What do you want with me?

HOLMES. I've come to take you up on your kind offer.

MRS. DILBER. My offer?

HOLMES. Yes. For a seance. I wish to speak to the dead. You see, I need a word with Ebenezer Scrooge.

MRS. DILBER. You wanna talk with Ol' Scratch, do ye? Why you wanna do that?

HOLMES. There are many questions which need answers. And I understand spirits quite enjoy coming to this house on Christmas Eve.

MRS. DILBER. You don't wanna be messing round willy-nilly with things ye don't understand, sir. I don't wish to contact any ghosts tonight, thankee very much.

HOLMES. Nevertheless, I'll need you to try. You did say Scrooge had not yet crossed over. Perhaps he is here in this very room with us now.

Thunder rumbles. Holmes uses his candle to look about. He speaks with a sense of excited curiosity.

And what might he say, if we asked him about the missing will—and to whom he intended to give the Blue Carbuncle?

MRS. DILBER. I'm sure I don't know.

HOLMES. Perhaps not. But what might Scrooge say about the note that was sent to him—the threat on his life?

MRS. DILBER. Terrible business, now, if you don't mind...?

Holmes places the candle in an empty candleholder from the mantle and holds it up.

HOLMES. And finally, just how, exactly, did he die? Perhaps, we can ask him all that. And more. About the past. The present. And especially the future.

MRS. DILBER. I think I've heard quite enough of this blither blather, Detective.

Holmes sits in Scrooge's wheelchair. He holds the candle delicately.

HOLMES. And so we have set our scene. Tell me, how do we do this, now, Mrs. Dilber? You are the conduit, after all. I've heard we need an object that belonged to the deceased, this chair will do...

and a candle. I think we have the perfect candle, don't you? Such a strong aroma.

Mrs. Dilber runs to the door. It is locked. She breathes hard.

Yes, the door is locked. So that the spirit cannot escape. The window is bolted, too.

MRS. DILBER. Open the door. Open the bleedin' door, I tell you.

HOLMES. I will not. In fact, that door will not be opened until you make Scrooge appear and all of our questions are answered.

MRS. DILBER. You have to let me out of here. Right now.

HOLMES. I am prepared to stay here as long as it takes.

MRS. DILBER. You don't understand!

HOLMES. Oh, I think I do. We will sit here together until this candle burns to the nub.

She races to a candle to blow it out. Holmes evades her.

MRS. DILBER. Blow out that candle. Blow it out I say!

The wind picks up with a distant, haunting moan.

HOLMES. But why? Quite pungent. Just like the scent I noted this morning. Mr. Burke told me Scrooge's candles were custom-made, the scent provided by the customer. Reminds me a bit of your cake, now, doesn't it? Your famous chocolate amaretto. Smells like almonds.

MRS. DILBER. We cannot stay in here, please!

HOLMES. But of course the cake was stale when I arrived, wasn't it? But then if the cake was not freshly baked on these premises, what accounted for the overwhelming scent, like burnt almonds?

MRS. DILBER. Here now, sir. Don't scare me like this! I gots a weak pumper, you know.

HOLMES. Yes! I'm a bit nervous, too. Though I'm a skeptic, I find I am beginning to believe… With every passing moment, I feel Mr. Scrooge drawing nearer. Don't you? Oh yes, I feel him, now.

Thunder rumbles. She backs up.

MRS. DILBER. Mr. Holmes, I was only foolin'. There's no such thing as ghosts. Forget the seance. Forget Scrooge.

HOLMES. Forget Scrooge? I could never. There's much to learn from his story. He changed his ways. He solved life's greatest mysteries. Like any good detective, he sought out the truth. You know what the truth is, don't you? Because I do. The truth is that it was you Mrs. Dilber...

> *A whispered voice calls. The candle flutters. Holmes does not notice.*

SCROOGE'S VOICE. *Mrs. Dilber...*

HOLMES. It was you who wanted Scrooge dead.

MRS. DILBER. You're mad.

> *Holmes barrels through the following accusations quickly— he is his old self and has rediscovered his joy in solving a case!*

HOLMES. You didn't retire last year. Mr. Scrooge fired you rather than reporting you to the police. He let you keep your reputation. You were stealing from him. Little trinkets. Spoons, with a fanciful "S" for instance. You pawned them at Old Joe's.

MRS. DILBER. Mr. Holmes, the candle—

HOLMES. Oh yes. The custom-made scented candles which lined these walls. The candles which Henry Burke unwittingly made at your request. They contained a rather special ingredient to give them their scent. Didn't they? An ingredient which smells distinctly like burning almonds. These candles are made with cyanide.

MRS. DILBER. Don't be a fool, man.

HOLMES. Cyanide which you stole from Doctor Cratchit's cabinet at St. Bernard's Children's Hospital. There was a break-in there last Tuesday, I believe. The same day you volunteer.

MRS. DILBER. I had nothing to do with that!

HOLMES. Really now, Mrs. Dilber. Stealing from children? It's almost enough to make one say—

SCROOGE'S VOICE. *BAAAAAH. HUMMMBUUGGGG...*

HOLMES. Bah, humbug.

MRS. DILBER. Did you hear that?

HOLMES. I may have. I'm not sure. It might all be in my head. These candles do make one a bit woozy. Does it matter? What matters is that Mr. Scrooge was to receive the Carbuncle as a gift from the Countess of Morcar. You thought he had it already, and you knew this house's hiding places better than anyone. If you could only find it, you could make off with the diamond and sell it. Mr. Scrooge having been so frail of late, you sent him a threatening note, hoping to scare him, perhaps weaken his heart—

SCROOGE'S VOICE. "YoUr GhoSts HavE ReTurNed."

MRS. DILBER. What's that?

HOLMES. But the Old Man was strong. He was not scared by the note, its cuttings made by—

> *He picks up the magnifying glass on the table and throws it at her. She catches it with her left hand, startled.*

A left-handed person trying to appear right-handed.

MRS. DILBER. Oh Lord.

> *And now, Holmes drives it home, with a flair for the dramatic.*

HOLMES. You arrived here after dark, last evening, when Scrooge was asleep. You needed time to let the cyanide candles burn down. You found Scrooge in his chair, struck a match, locked him in his room and waited for him to die. Fannie Gardner came to the door at midnight. She saw Scrooge through the window, but didn't have the courage to knock. You were safe, for the moment.

But, you didn't count on Tiny Tim.

You were here when he arrived in the morning. And you were forced to discover the body with Dr. Cratchit present. He noted the door locked from the outside, which aroused in him suspicions of foul play. But if there had been a murder, where was the weapon? Cleverly melted down, the poison having done its work on the man, whom anyone might have thought died from old age. The authorities wouldn't find any marks on the body and given that it was Christmas, an autopsy would be postponed for a day. By that time any trace of cyanide in the body would be gone, a unique property of the poison. When Cratchit went to fetch Lestrade, you scrubbed the wax drippings from the floor to destroy any evidence. A housekeeper to the end. It was you, Mrs. Dilber...

SCROOGE'S VOICE. *Mrs. Dilber...*

HOLMES. It was you!

She turns cold, hard.

MRS. DILBER. And what if it was? What if I did do all what you said? The ol' humbug. I don't care if he was a changed man.

All I ever got was a little raise each Christmas and the promise I'd always have my job. You think I wanted to be his housekeeper me whole life? And him handing out money to every portly gentleman and sorry soul comes his way.

So, maybe I stole a fancy spoon or a set of bed curtains to hock. What of it? That Blue Carbuncle wasn't ever going to me, now, was it? So I had to make sure it would!

HOLMES. And without a will, who could contest if you claimed he gave it to you... But you could find neither the will, nor this diamond.

He holds out the diamond. She gasps in feverish desire.

MRS. DILBER. How'd you get that?

HOLMES. I went on a wild goose chase. This candle is starting to affect my senses, Mrs. Dilber. Can you feel it, too?

MRS. DILBER. I'll say you broke in here and stole that diamond. Threatened to poison me with cyanide. The police'd believe that. Even that pigeon-livered bungler Lestrade would buy it! Everyone knows you ain't exactly been y'self lately, you malmsey-nosed blunderbus.

And 'sides, I'm not afraid of you. So long as I'm locked in here with that candle burning, so are you.

HOLMES. Quite right.

Holmes blows out the candle. Thunder and lightning.

MRS. DILBER. What's this?

SCROOGE'S VOICE. *Mrs. Dilber...*

Scrooge appears in a flash of light. Dilber screams. Scrooge disappears.

Dilber panics. Is she alone in the room? She looks about. She turns around and is face-to-face with Holmes.

MRS. DILBER. He's here. He's in this room. I saw him. I saw him! It was Scrooge! Ebenezer Scrooge! He's come for me.

HOLMES. I knew he'd show up.

MRS. DILBER. Let me out of here!

> *Mrs. Dilber rushes to the door, which opens forcefully as Lestrade bursts in with a bobby (Actor One) close behind.*

LESTRADE. Gladly, madame! Heard the whole thing at the keyhole, Mr. Holmes. Every last word of her confession. Pigeon-livered, am I? It was all just as you said! Wasn't it, sir?

MRS. DILBER. Take me away, Inspector. I admit it! I'm the murderer! But take me from this 'orrible, 'aunted place! He was here. He was here!

LESTRADE. Was he, now?

MRS. DILBER. You know now, Mr. Holmes, don't you?

HOLMES. Know what?

MRS. DILBER. There are such things…as ghosts.

LESTRADE. Take her away, Constable Bradstreet.

CONSTABLE. Yes, sir! Right this way, ma'am.

MRS. DILBER. Yes! Thank you, thank you! *(Mildly flirty with Bradstreet.)* Take me, please!

> *The constable takes Mrs. Dilber from the room.*

LESTRADE. What's she going on about, then, Mr. Holmes? What's all this business about ghosts?

HOLMES. I'm sure I don't know. Perhaps she really saw one. Who is to say?

LESTRADE. Surely you don't believe in ghosts, now. Do you?

HOLMES. I prefer the term Spirit. Which is something Ebenezer Scrooge had in abundance.

LESTRADE. Indeed. Awful to think a kindly man like that would meet such an end. Murdered. On Christmas Eve, no less.

> *Holmes chuckles.*

HOLMES. Oh, Scrooge wasn't murdered, Lestrade.

LESTRADE. But you said there was a murderer on the loose!

HOLMES. And there was. But that didn't mean a murder had been committed.
Don't you remember? We found Mr. Scrooge in his chair reading a newspaper dated December 22. Rigor had clearly set in. The

room was quite cold and it preserved him, as he sat here with a smile on his lips.

LESTRADE. So Scrooge…?

HOLMES. Died three days ago. On his birthday. Quite peacefully, too. A life well lived.

Lestrade is astounded!

LESTRADE. So the poison candles didn't kill him!

HOLMES. They never would have.

LESTRADE. What do y'mean?

HOLMES. Oh, really Lestrade. Poisoned candles? It's the most ridiculous scheme I've ever heard of. Utterly absurd. Never would have worked, though they might make you hallucinate a bit. But you'd have to practically eat the candles to have them prove fatal.

LESTRADE. So, the housekeeper tried to commit murder against a man who had already passed away!

HOLMES. Mrs. Dilber isn't exactly a criminal mastermind.

LESTRADE. Well, they can't all be Professor Moriartys, now, can they?

HOLMES. Thank goodness.

LESTRADE. Scrooge went out on his own terms, didn't he?

HOLMES. He was a brave soul. He chose to change his ways and do good for his fellow man. His example is a gift to us all.

LESTRADE. And speaking of gifts, I guess we'll never know what happened to Scrooge's will!

HOLMES. Oh, I have it right here.

Holmes produces the will.

LESTRADE. Ha! Where'd you find that, then?

HOLMES. In the safe. Behind the portrait of his sister, Fan. Anything he truly valued he would have kept close to her—the person he most cherished.

LESTRADE. And how'd you open the safe?

HOLMES. The combination was simple. 3-6-4.

He mimes turning the combination.

The exact number of gifts given in "The Twelve Days of Christmas," Scrooge's favorite carol. "It all adds up," as he might say.

LESTRADE. So, do you know who the Blue Carbuncle goes to?

HOLMES. I do, sir. I do! Quite a gift. A remarkable gift, indeed!

Church bells chime. Lestrade is caught up in Holmes' delight.

LESTRADE. It's midnight!

HOLMES. A new day.

LESTRADE. Christmas Day, Mr. Holmes. It's Christmas!

The company strikes Scrooge's study. Holmes puts on something a bit more festive, looking like his old self, with a sprig of holly in his lapel and a colorful scarf. A jaunty Christmas carol plays. Sleigh bells ring.

ACTOR ONE. And indeed it was.

ACTOR THREE. The next morning was Christmas Morning. The most wonderful time of the year.

ACTOR ONE. The bells chimed loud in old St. Stephen's.

ACTOR THREE. The snow lay round about. Deep and crisp and even.

ACTOR ONE. Along Baker Street the good people of London rejoiced to see their neighbor—

ACTOR THREE. The Great Sherlock Holmes—

HOLMES. The World's Foremost Consulting Detective!

ACTOR ONE. Was back on the case!

HOLMES. The game is afoot! It's always afoot!

Actor One puts on his cap. He is Cratchit.

CRATCHIT. *(Astonished.)* Mr. Holmes. I heard about Mrs. Dilber. We owe you a great deal.

HOLMES. It is I who owe you, sir! I come with tidings of comfort and joy, Doctor. Mr. Scrooge's will has been found. And it specifies you as the recipient of the Blue Carbuncle. It should fetch a handsome price and keep your doors open for years to come.

CRATCHIT. Oh, Mr. Holmes. Thank you!

HOLMES. Thank Mr. Scrooge.

Emma enters and hugs Holmes.

EMMA WIGGINS. Mr. Holmes. My father! He's been released! He's inside now! I have him back. He's free, sir, he's free!

HOLMES. I'd like to meet him, Emma. So I can tell him personally what a remarkable daughter he has in you.

EMMA WIGGINS. Thank you, sir.

She exits.

CRATCHIT. It's just like one of those stories in the *Strand*, Mr. Holmes. I don't know how you do it.

HOLMES. Elementary, my dear Cratchit. Elementary.

CRATCHIT. By the way, a letter arrived this morning. Someone knew you'd be here.

HOLMES. Miss Adler.

The Countess appears, elsewhere.

THE COUNTESS. Dear Sherlock,

If you're reading this, you've solved the mystery, recaptured the diamond, and read Ebenezer's will. The Blue Carbuncle has found its rightful home, and you have saved the day. I shall return to London in a year's time, at Christmas. Perhaps then, we can make up for lost time and sing a few carols of our own. Until then, I remain yours, Irene Adler,

HOLMES. The Countess of Morcar.

The Countess disappears.

CRATCHIT. Now then, will you join us inside for Christmas?

HOLMES. Thank you, Doctor. But I'm afraid I can't stay. I have an appointment to keep. With an old friend.

Watson enters. He has on an apron and is rushing about at home.

WATSON. Take over stirring, Mary! I'll see to the door. It's probably just the neighbor wondering if we're—

He sees Sherlock, who holds a wrapped bottle in hand.

Holmes.

HOLMES. If your invitation stands, I should like to come to dinner, after all.

WATSON. Well, yes. Of course. Come in, come in.

HOLMES. This is for you.

WATSON. A Christmas Spirit?

HOLMES. A Christmas Present. I should have come sooner, but somehow, I lost my way.

WATSON. You needn't apologize.

HOLMES. Yesterday, I said a great many things I regret. I'm sorry I disappointed you. I won't do it again. You have my word.

WATSON. It's all right, old man. It's all right.

HOLMES. So I still have your friendship?

WATSON. Sherlock. You never lost it.

HOLMES. That's the greatest gift of all, John.

WATSON. But what about Moriarty's ghost?

HOLMES. Oh, I don't think I shall worry about Moriarty anymore. We have bigger cases to tackle. Together. As Holmes and Watson.

WATSON. May I ask what caused your change of heart?

HOLMES. I solved a mystery, Watson. You see there was a man named Scrooge who—

WATSON. Ebenezer Scrooge?

HOLMES. Yes, did you know him?

WATSON. When I was just a boy. The meanest old fusser on the street. Everyone was afraid of him. Until one Christmas morning I saw him at his window, shouting—

SCROOGE. You there! Young boy! What day is this?

Watson acts within his recollection.

WATSON. Why it's Christmas Day, sir!

SCROOGE. Christmas Day? I haven't missed it! The Spirits have done it all in one night. Of course they have! Oh my fine boy, do you know the poultry shop on the corner?

WATSON. I do, sir!

SCROOGE. Intelligent boy! Remarkable boy! Go and fetch the turkey hanging in their window!

WATSON. The one as big as me, sir?

SCROOGE. Indeed! I'll send it to Bob Cratchit! I'll give you a shilling—no two shillings—if you're quick about it!

WATSON. Right, sir! Merry Christmas, sir!

SCROOGE. Merry Christmas, indeed! Merry Christmas everyone! Ha ha!

WATSON. And from that day on he was a changed man.

HOLMES. Quite a story.

WATSON. Yes, a Dickens of a tale. Told many times and many ways, but I never tire of it.

> *Watson picks up a wrapped box.*

Oh, Holmes, before I forget, here's a little something for you, too.

> *He hands Holmes a present, which is unwrapped quickly. It's—*

HOLMES. A deerstalker. Why, Watson. However did you guess?

WATSON. Will you wear it?

HOLMES. As if my life depended upon it.

WATSON. Merry Christmas, Holmes.

HOLMES. Merry Christmas, Watson.

> *Some music plays from inside. "We Wish You a Merry Christmas."*

Shall we go inside and sing?

WATSON. Sherlock Holmes and a Christmas carol? Now, I've seen everything!

HOLMES. So you have, Watson. So you have.

ACTOR TWO. And so have you!

SCROOGE. Sherlock Holmes had no further visits by ghosts.

HOLMES. And he was better than his word.

ACTOR TWO. He did it all and infinitely more.

ACTOR THREE. He became as good a friend—

ACTOR FOUR. As good a man—

ACTOR ONE. As good a detective—

ACTOR THREE. As this good old city ever knew.

HOLMES. It was all quite—elementary!

SCROOGE. For as Tiny Tim once said—
CRATCHIT. God Bless us, everyone!
> *A Christmas tree is revealed. It is crowned with a star—the Blue Carbuncle! It snows as if from heaven!*

ALL.
> *We wish you a Merry Christmas and a Happy New Year!*
> *The players bow and exit the stage in celebration! It's Christmas!*

Fin.

PROPERTY LIST
(Use this space to create props lists for your production)

SOUND EFFECTS
(Use this space to create sound effects lists for your production)

Hello, actors, theatre makers, and theatre fans,

On behalf of the Broadway Licensing Group and the author(s) of this work, we thank you for your continued support of the arts and the playwrights you love.

Like every title in our catalogue, this play is covered by copyright law, which ensures authors are rewarded for creating new dramatic work and protects them from theft and abuse of their work. We are compelled to impress upon all who obtain this edition that **this text may not be copied, distributed, or publicly produced in any way**, nor uploaded to any file-sharing websites or software—public or private. Any such action has an immediate and negative effect on the livelihood of the writer(s)—it is also stealing and is against the law. As a result, should you copy, distribute, or publicly produce any part of this text without express written consent and licensed permission from our company—even if no one is being paid and/or admission is not being charged—your organization shall be subject to legal consequences that we are sure you want to avoid.

But we have faith in you and your understanding of these guidelines!

While this acting edition is the only approved text for performance, there may be other editions of the play available for sale. It is important to note that our team has worked with the playwright(s) to ensure this published acting edition reflects their desired text for all future productions. If you have purchased a revised edition from us, that is the only edition you may use for performance, unless explicitly stated in writing by our team.

Finally, and this is an important one, **this script cannot be changed in any way** without written permission from our team. That said, feel free to reach out to us. We don't bite, and we are always happy to have a discussion to see if we can accommodate your request.

We are thrilled this play has made it into your hands and we hope you love it as much as we do. Thank you for helping us keep the theatre alive and well, and for supporting playwrights, in our continued journey to make everyone a theatre person!

Sincerely,
Fellow theatre lovers at the Broadway Licensing Group

Note on Songs/Recordings, Images, or Other Production Design Elements

Be advised that Broadway Licensing neither holds the rights to nor grants permission to use any songs, recordings, images, or other design elements mentioned in the play. It is the responsibility of the producing theater/organization to obtain permission of the copyright owner(s) for any such use. Additional royalty fees may apply for the right to use copyrighted materials.

For any songs/recordings, images, or other design elements mentioned in the play, works in the public domain may be substituted. It is the producing theater/organization's responsibility to ensure the substituted work is indeed in the public domain. Broadway Licensing cannot advise as to whether or not a song/arrangement/recording, image, or other design element is in the public domain.